# AMERICAN HERITAGE

*October, 1971 · Volume XXII, Number 6*

*Burning Zenger's papers*

# LETTER FROM THE EDITOR

Much of the history we present in this magazine seems, as a child might say, "all over." The stories are concluded, the dead buried. The settings tend to become variously "shrines" or restorations—although, as the venturers on our new American Heritage Society tours have been noticing, in privileged peeks beyond the velvet ropes, these monuments also change, along with our views of history. Looking through this issue, one might observe that the GI's of other times, caricatured so deftly by Peter Copeland, have all tossed their last sloppy salute; that the polluting horses are gone at last from our cities; that the lonely, insecure little niece of Theodore Roosevelt "found romance" (as they say in the women's magazines) in an affecting Victorian way, married her fifth cousin, and became, whatever you thought of her, a Formidable Lady. And died. It is, as the child said, all over.

Or perhaps not. Our soldiers and sailors today have new problems of discipline, morale, and drugs, and want to change their uniforms. As for the horse as an urban polluter, have you heard about the automobile? And Eleanor Roosevelt, the shy debutante who became the Social Force, did she not stir up the minorities, the "underprivileged," and even Women's Lib? And did she not marry the man, "that man," who hated war, and would not send our sons into one—but did?

Separating past and present, in other words, grows complicated. Just as we were getting ready for our next issue a detailed article on the trial of John Peter Zenger in 1735, that first American landmark in the battle for the freedom of the press, the issue came up again—the very same principle—in the case of the *New York Times* and other newspapers that had begun publishing the now famous Pentagon Papers. With their revelations from documents of the Defense Department, the National Security Council, and other sources they traced a very different picture of our growing involvement in Vietnam than that set forth in public by several Presidents and their spokesmen. Here, for example, was President Johnson addressing the people on September 25, 1964:

"There are those who say, you ought to go north and drop bombs. . . . We don't want our American boys to do the fighting for Asian boys. We don't want to get involved in a nation with 700 million people and get tied down in a land war in Asia."

Privately, as the *Times* summary of the Pentagon study revealed:

"The Johnson Administration reached a 'general consensus' at a White House strategy meeting on Sept. 7, 1964, that air attacks against North Vietnam would probably have to be launched, [the Pentagon study] states . . . 'What prevented action for the time being was a set of tactical considerations.' The first tactical consideration, the analyst says, was that 'the President was in the midst of an election campaign in which he was presenting himself as the candidate of reason and restraint

as opposed to the quixotic Barry Goldwater,' who was publicly advocating full-scale bombing of North Vietnam."

For any reader who has not been away on the moon or marooned in a mine, we scarcely need rehearse all the other secrets brought out, or the arguments about them. Nor do we need to remind the historically minded that there is nothing new to all this. Lyndon Johnson, like Franklin Roosevelt before him, was, to put it mildly, less than frank with the public—and so in their times, on the same issue of going to war, were William McKinley (who did not choose to reveal that the Spanish had already given in as he called for a declaration of war) and, for another example, James K. Polk (as he manipulated his way into war with Mexico). It did help, in these earlier cases, that we won the wars. Victory has a powerful effect on the reputations of Commanders in Chief.

Leaving aside truly genuine matters of security, which the courts in the *New York Times* case found were not an issue, a historian must conclude that politicians have a right to secrets, if they can keep them, and newspapers have a right to reveal them, if they can find them. It is a game, if you will, for all the moralizing. It is for this reason, foreseen by our prescient Founding Fathers, that the very first amendment to the Constitution guarantees the press a special freedom as a kind of tribune of the people to keep the government honest. Its task, to put it crudely, is to keep the outsiders informed about what the rascally insiders are doing.

The historian, whom we must assume for a moment to be an honest searcher after truth—a large assumption to be sure—cannot fully trust anyone, or else his subject would not continually be in the process of revision. He cannot keep a closed mind, like the simple patriot who cries "treason" at all who disagree with him, as indeed some have done in the case of the *Times*. The historian has to remember that treason is relative, that one season's rebel is another's loyalist, and that consistency is a rarity. Even the righteous *Times* not so long ago was thundering "breach of security" at two reporters, Stewart Alsop and Charles Bartlett, for their revelations in the *Saturday Evening Post* about what went on within the Kennedy administration during the Cuban missile crisis.

One may be permitted a fleeting smile at the way in which 1962's "breach of security" becomes 1971's sacred duty to history, but one must also admit that editorial writers, if anonymous, are human, and that the accumulation of disasters in our time has been enough to change anyone's mind. To get back to our opening point, it would be comforting if any important part of history could safely be pasted into some kind of national scrapbook, labelled "The Settled Past," and put away. But that is impossible as long as people keep records—especially if they mark them "burn this letter," or "top secret." That makes their reappearance as certain as that of Banquo's ghost, and as troubling. All over? Never.
—*Oliver Jensen*

# AMERICAN HERITAGE

*The Magazine of History*

SENIOR EDITOR
Bruce Catton

EDITOR
Oliver Jensen

ARTICLES EDITOR
E. M. Halliday

EXECUTIVE EDITOR
Nat Brandt

ASSOCIATE EDITORS
Barbara Klaw        Bernard A. Weisberger

ART DIRECTOR
Emma Landau

PICTURE EDITORS
Carla Davidson        Mary Dawn Earley

COPY EDITOR
Joyce O'Connor

ASSISTANT: Devorah Kanter

CONSULTING EDITOR: Joan Paterson Kerr

CONTRIBUTING EDITOR: Robert C. Alberts

ADVISORY BOARD
Carl Carmer                    Eric F. Goldman
Gerald Carson                  Louis C. Jones
Henry Steele Commager          Alvin M. Josephy, Jr.
Marshall B. Davidson           Howard H. Peckham
John A. Garraty                Francis S. Ronalds
S. K. Stevens

AMERICAN HERITAGE PUBLISHING CO., INC.

PRESIDENT AND PUBLISHER
Paul Gottlieb

EDITOR IN CHIEF
Joseph J. Thorndike

SENIOR EDITOR
Richard M. Ketchum

EDITORIAL ART DIRECTOR
Murray Belsky

AMERICAN HERITAGE is published every two months by American Heritage Publishing Co., Inc.; editorial and executive offices, 551 Fifth Avenue, New York, N.Y. 10017. Treasurer, Marjorie C. Dyer; Secretary, John C. Taylor III. Correspondence about subscriptions should be sent to American Heritage Subscription Office, 383 West Center Street, Marion, Ohio 43302. Single copies: $5.00. Annual subscriptions: $20.00 in U.S. and Canada; $21.00 elsewhere.

A ten-year Index covering Volumes VI–XV is available at $5.00, and a five-year Index of Volumes XVI–XX at $3.50.

AMERICAN HERITAGE will consider but assumes no responsibility for unsolicited materials. Title registered U.S. Patent Office. Second-class postage paid at New York, N.Y., and at additional mailing offices.

*Sponsored by*
American Association for State & Local History · Society of American Historians

## CONTENTS *October, 1971 · Volume XXII, Number 6*

COVERS: The caricatures on both our covers serve to introduce a portfolio, beginning on the next page, of Peter Copeland's humorous studies of early American uniforms; we think them a wonderful reversal of the clichés common to this art form. Yet the military details are accurate. His Puritan militiaman on the front cover carries a matchlock, a long smouldering wick for igniting his charge, a forked rest to support the barrel, and a kind of bandoleer of a dozen wooden containers of premeasured charges of powder known as the Twelve Disciples. If all fails (and it often did), he has a sword. The bo's'n on the back cover, advancing menacingly on his men with belaying pin in hand, dates back to just before the era when dress for seamen and noncommissioned officers was standardized. In selecting his hat this lovable character has taken full advantage of his privileges.

*T*he American provincials looked ridiculous. They had no military bearing. Their formations were ragged, and they argued with their officers. Sometimes they were so clumsy they made the regulars of the British army highly nervous—and with good cause. Like the time in 1758 when some of the Massachusetts men with General James Abercromby's army in the campaign against Fort Ticonderoga were given permission to clear the charges from their muzzle-loading muskets by firing them off. "There was a fine fiering of them for a spael," reported Amos Richardson of Woburn, "and some of ouer men Did Shut one of the Reglers Throu the Head which killed hem Daed." It is no wonder the British sometimes felt it was safer to face the French than accept the aid of their American friends. Well before this, about 1755, if tradition is to be believed, Dr. Richard Shuckburgh had expressed the redcoats' derision of American soldiers by writing "Yankee Doodle" and setting it to an old British tune.

When Lord Percy marched out of Boston to rescue the British force that had struck a hornet's nest at Concord on April 19, 1775, his musicians played the song in derision, but they fell silent on their nightmare retreat. And the tune took on entirely new meanings when victorious

# DRESS PARADE

## A PORTFOLIO OF AMERICAN FIGHTING MEN

Americans played it as they marched into Boston, and later as one British army surrendered at Saratoga and another at Yorktown. The country bumpkins had triumphed over the best of the professionals, and they had accompanied victory with a self-deriding song.

In a real sense "Yankee Doodle" set a style for the way America's nonprofessional warriors have regarded themselves ever since. Far from resenting the jibes at their amateur status, they have gloried in them. Unlike most other world powers, the United States has never had an elite military caste. In times of emergency all able-bodied males have been expected to serve their country. For that reason the outlook of the average fighting man has remained essentially that of a civilian, and he has been quick to note the anomalies of his position and the idiosyncrasies of his fellows.

Perhaps it is this attitude that has produced an American military humor that is in many ways unique. When the soldier is Everyman, the humorist's laugh is really on himself and is seldom very bitter. Our jibes began early, as in R. H. Hobson's 1829 cartoon *The Nation's Bulwark—A Well Disciplined Militia*, which depicts a motley and slightly inebriated rank of heroes. Americans have welcomed the gentle thumb pricks of Winslow Homer and identified wholeheartedly with Edward Streeter's "Bill" in World War I and with George Baker's "Sad Sack" and Bill Mauldin's "Willie" and "Joe" in World War II.

The men cited above were dealing with the present, while the artist represented on these pages is looking at the past. The essence of caricature is exaggeration, and here it is in full fettle: the high stiff collar that keeps a soldier from turning his head, the impressive cap falling over the eye, the determined—if baffled—expression, and the somewhat less than heroic physique. Dealing in this humorous way with history requires not only a thorough knowledge of dress and weapons, but a happily jaundiced eye as well. Fortunately, the artist Peter Copeland has them both. One of the nation's leading students of costume, both military and civilian, he has served in the merchant marine during World War II and the Korean conflict, and in the Army in 1955–57. He has also done a stint as a combat artist in Vietnam. But he has remained a civilian iconoclast, and he joins a long line of self-deprecating citizen-warriors stemming from the patriots who first heard in the comic notes of "Yankee Doodle" a viable statement about American military life.

*Water colors by*
PETER COPELAND

*Text by*
HAROLD L. PETERSON

*A private, Sherburne's Regiment, Continental Army, 1779*

During the Revolution the rifleman caught the public eye, while his infantry brother, who did the bulk of the fighting, was largely ignored. Following the war, militiamen all over the new nation formed themselves into rifle units in imitation of their lionized predecessors. New York State ended up with a whole corps of riflemen, such as the private of 1809 at left, who served as a handsome, fierce-looking escort for the governor. When the War of 1812 came, some of these unfortunates had to fight, and many also had to give up their treasured rifles and carry muskets just like the common infantryman of the day.

Light or horse artillery were the elite of cannoneers. The dashing young men, mounted on swift horses, moved into (and out of) action with élan. In 1808 the United States decided to establish a regiment of ten companies with special uniform caps, short coats, and jackboots. It bought horses for one company, which then made a heroic march (at the rate of six miles an hour) from Baltimore to Washington. Official ardor subsequently cooled, and the horses for the other companies never appeared. As a result the would-be horse artillerymen had to serve as infantry until the War of 1812. Even the one lucky company lost its horses, in 1809. The elegant number-one matross at left below has apparently just gotten the word.

The War of 1812 brought laurels to the young American Navy. In battle after battle its upstart seamen won victories over the ships of the world's greatest naval power. In these bloody encounters officers and men wore utilitarian garments, but there was another side of naval life. Every ship must spend some time in port, and here the gallant officer had a chance to prove his prowess in different encounters. These activities required a far finer dress. What belle could refuse a dance with the captain at right?

"War is sweet to those that have never experienced it," says Pindar. In the years of peace from 1815 to 1846 military life appealed to thousands of American males, who could dress in fancy uniforms, camp out in good weather, fire muskets or cannon, and imbibe huge quantities of ferociously potent punches. Militia units mushroomed all over the country, naming themselves after national heroes, localities, even colors. There was glory for all—and no danger. The spreading hero, left, belongs to the Washington Grays of Philadelphia.

The 1840's found the Navy active in many endeavors—exploring the Isthmus of Panama, visiting the Arctic and the Antarctic, raising the American flag over the landlocked Sea of Galilee. Our brave tars even fought in California (seizing Monterey a bit prematurely, before any war had begun). The year 1842 was a bad one, however, because it witnessed a cut in the cherished grog ration from the traditional eight ounces to a measly four—and seamen under twenty-one got none at all. But the sailor at left below has already learned the practical benefits of private enterprise.

By definition dragoons, like the trooper at right, were supposed to be soldiers equally at home on horseback or afoot, and "always ready on every emergency." By 1848 the Army boasted three regiments of them. They had fought dismounted through the swamps of The Everglades and had tried to contain the Indians of the Plains on horseback. Dragoons were authorized two uniforms: a spectacular dress outfit for adding color to ceremonies and the slightly less showy garb worn in this painting. For fighting afoot this fearless warrior has the latest breechloading Hall carbine, and for mounted combat he wears the model 1840 saber, which was known affectionately to its users as the "old Wrist-breaker."

*Cavalrymen, like this sergeant of 1863 at left, have always had a certain air about them, although in the opening years of the Civil War the federal cavalry indeed did very little of note. They scouted a bit, carried messages, ran from Confederate horsemen, and led the good life. "Who ever saw a dead cavalryman?" General Joe Hooker asked. But later they did handsomely.*

*Virginians prided themselves on their horsemanship, and volunteer cavalry units were many, like the Sussex Light Dragoons of 1861. One proud trooper of that unit is shown at the bottom left.*

*At right we have another mean old Reb, a private in the Rough and Ready Guards of North Carolina in 1861. The Old North State claims it supplied more men and took heavier casualties than any other in the Confederacy. One of the units that helped establish both these records was this one, under the captaincy of the renowned Zebulon Vance, who characterized himself as "awfully rough but scarcely ever ready."*

## A NOTE TO MEMBERS OF THE AMERICAN HERITAGE SOCIETY

**These whimsical caricatures are selected from *America's Fighting Men*, a portfolio of twenty-four prints from paintings by Peter Copeland of the Smithsonian Institution. It will be published this month by the New York Graphic Society in a limited, de luxe edition of one thousand signed and numbered sets, at $100 a set. In addition to the twenty-four prints, each 10 by 13 inches in size, the boxed portfolio includes a sixty-four page book, bound and gold stamped, containing a preface and historical notations by Harold L. Peterson, chief curator of the National Park Service and former president of the Company of Military Historians. Any American Heritage Society member who would like to acquire a set may write for information to Mr. Martin Rapp, American Heritage Publishing Co., Inc., 551 Fifth Avenue, New York City, New York 10017.**

# THE SWAY OF THE

By JOHN MALCOLM BRINNIN

## "THIS IS NOT A CANOE"

*Der Doppelschrauben Schnelldampfer Kronprinzessin Cecilie,* loaded with about eleven million dollars' worth of gold and silver bullion and more than one thousand passengers, was halfway from New York to Plymouth, en route to Bremerhaven. On the night of July 31, 1914, the man on duty in the little shack on deck that housed the wireless was subjected to an intense crackling on his ear set. "Urgent and Confidential . . . Urgent

and Confidential," followed by a message addressed to the ship's captain: "Erhard has suffered attack of catarrh of the bladder. Siegfried." The Marconi man at once took this message to the bridge. Captain Polack—"our precious Polack" to many Americans who had known him since the days, twenty years before, when he was second officer on another German liner, the *Spree*—recognized it as instructions in code, a

code he had earlier been supplied with the means to decipher.

The burden of the message was twofold: war was about to be declared between the Central and Allied powers; the captain was to take every precaution to prevent the capture of his ship—Germany's most famous liner—by the British. He ordered the course of the *Kronprinzessin Cecilie* to be reversed, then grandly descended to the grand saloon that

# GRAND SALOON

In the sumptuous history of transatlantic passenger travel it wasn't all mahogany panelling and ten-course meals. Consider, for instance, war and seasickness

*When Bar Harbor residents awoke on the morning of August 4, 1914, they were astonished to see an enormous ocean liner anchored in the cozy port, parallel to Bar Harbor's lacy landmark, the Reading Room pier. Most people assumed the hastily disguised ship was British.*

was ornamented with paintings representing "ideal" landscapes—motifs from the gardens of the Italian Renaissance palaces of Lante, Farnese, Palmieri, Gorgoni, Albani, Doria, Borghese, and d'Este, and from the Vatican gardens. He silenced an orchestra playing for an after-dinner dance and summoned a few socially prominent individuals among the passengers to join him in that "acme of cosiness," the *Rauch-zimmer* ("smoking room"). There, as the player piano waited for someone to pump out "The Whistler and His Dog" or "The Skater's Waltz," the chosen few lit cigars beneath busts of Apollo and Minerva. "Gentlemen," the captain said, "it is my duty to inform you that I have orders from the Imperial German Government to take this ship to a neutral port in the United States."

In no time at all the word had spread to the Vienna Café (where a single à la carte meal cost just about as much as a steerage passage ticket for the whole crossing), to the wind shelters on deck—"an ingenious invention of Director von Helmholt, of Bremen, which has been patented in all civilized states"—to the Imperial suites with their dining and drawing rooms, to the nether regions of the ship where hearty German-Americans played cards in the dim light of barren lounges or slept off big dinners in their iron bunks. In spite of general consternation and disbelief, anyone with an eye to see could tell that the backtracking of the great liner was already a *fait accompli*: the moon that had lately shone on the starboard was now coldly eyeing the port.

Captain Polack, assuring his passengers that their ship had ample fuel and food to bring them safely into port, asked them "to keep their heads." Most passengers accepted the circumstance, since there was nothing else to be done anyway. But for men of affairs dismay was unrelieved and desperate. Among the first-class passengers were American executives on financial missions, United States senators en route to an international conference, a large shooting party on the way to Scotland for the grouse. The most affluent of these got together and made up a purse. Then, ready to plunk their cash on the barrelhead, they went to Captain Polack. If he would replace the German imperial standard with the American flag, they said—and thus proceed in safety right under the bowsprits of the British Royal Navy—they would pay five million dollars for the ship and throw in a hefty bonus for the captain himself. The captain refused to be rescued by these Yankee plutocrats. He thanked them, had his ship's name blacked out, ordered black bands to be painted around the tops of her four yellowish funnels, and proceeded to carry out the instructions he had received from Berlin. His notion was to make his ship look, at least at a distance, like the four-funnelled *Olympic*, the British White Star liner.

In this naive disguise (almost everyone knew that funnels on German ships were placed in pairs, instead of equidistant, as on the British liners) the *Kronprinzessin* sped for the nearest American port. This, of all places, turned out to be Bar Harbor—and

at the very height of the season. The breakneck pace of the ship through fog and black of night made some passengers uneasy, some panicky. They chose a delegation and sent it to the captain begging him to slow down. But his only concession to their fears was a more liberal use of his foghorn. He knew what passengers did not: The French liner *La Savoie*, having discovered his position, had alerted the several French and

*The bemedalled Captain Charles Polack*
BROWN BROTHERS

British warships that were in a position to intercept the *Cecilie* and lay claim to her treasure-trove. Three nights after the dramatic turnabout, her portholes covered over with canvas, not a gleam of light along her length, the big ship, guided by the American yachtsman C. Ledyard Blair, who happened to be aboard, moseyed into Maine's Frenchman Bay and shut off her engines. A few hours later, early risers among the summer people looked out of their windows. There, riding at anchor among their own little flotilla of yachts and sailboats and Old Town canoes, they saw what most of them

took to be the great *Olympic*, sister ship of the *Titanic*.

The *Kronprinzessin* had "dropped her starboard anchor in the inner harbor about midway between the steamboat wharves and the Porcupines," said a local reporter. "The telephone operators were soon aware of her presence and those early upon the streets became excited as they learned of the presence here of the big German ship, and spread the news. By the middle of the forenoon the shore path was well covered with people and the [small boats] did a big business taking people out and back." By the time the resort had learned that its own gilt-and-wicker environs had provided safe haven for what the newspapers termed "the German gold ship," it had also learned of the unexpected return of two of its very own: Mrs. A. Howard Hinkle and her daughter, of Cincinnati, who were summer residents in one of Bar Harbor's big villas, did not disembark in Plymouth, England, but in their own back yard.

Faced with the option of internment in New England or capture by the British destroyers that were already hungrily cruising just beyond the international limit, Captain Polack chose to stay for the season. Bar Harbor suddenly became Fiddler's Green, the mythical sailor's heaven. (A good number of the resort's summer people knew the captain—"a moustachioed giant, over six feet tall" of "urbane charm and social graces"—because they had crossed on ships under his command.) The United States Coast Guard cutter *Androscoggin* had meanwhile sidled up to the *Kronprinzessin* and relieved her of her king's ransom in gold and silver bars. Special trains carried the bullion back to the vaults of New York's Guaranty Trust Company and the National Trust Company, from which, barely a week before, it had been removed for shipment to Germany.

Americans were still far enough

away from the war and partisan emotions to see the whole thing as a great sport. Almost at once Captain Polack and his officers became part of a summer's social whirl that saw them kissing the hands of hostesses at lawn parties, dancing at balls, going out on fishing and lobstering expeditions and sailing parties. A local man hired the Star movie theatre to entertain the *Kronprinzessin*'s crew; the ship's band gave concerts on the village green. Of the first of these the Bar Harbor *Record* reported:

A large crowd assembled to hear the music and showed their appreciation by their applause which in itself is most unusual for a crowd in Bar Harbor. For the last piece the band played *America*. This called for cheers and the blowing of horns by the large number of automobiles which had gathered to hear the music. The band then played *Watch on the Rhine*, which was so well received the crowd demanded an encore.

But soon upon these revels fell the shadow of the long arm of the law. Annoyed by the failure of the *Kronprinzessin* to deliver their gold bullion to Plymouth, the bankers concerned sued the North German Lloyd Steamship Company for damages in the amount of $1,040,467, plus interest. When this action was brought in the Bar Harbor Federal Court, doughty Deputy Marshal Eugene C. Harmon, according to the local paper, "left at noon to seize the ship." And he did.

Watched day and night by the cutter *Mohawk* and a torpedo boat, caught in the custodial web of the United States marshal for Maine, the great ship lay swinging at anchor late into the fall. With the approach of winter and the possible threat of ice damage, not only Captain Polack but his legal guardians were concerned to have the ship moved to a less hazardous anchorage. When a rumor was spread about that the *Kronprinzessin* might be taken to Portland, Bar Harbor was both angry and sad. The "ice charge" made its citizens furious; the possible loss of the ship made them prematurely nostalgic. Said the *Record*:

The streets of the town have been made interesting by the presence of the officers and the crew of the big liner, and Captain Polack has been the recipient of many social courtesies and has proven to be a most delightful gentleman as well as the notable and exceedingly efficient navigator he is known to be. Bar

*The* Cecilie *is relieved of her cargo—gold and silver ingots—by the U.S. Coast Guard.*

Harbor citizens have hoped that the big liner would stay here until the conclusion of the big European war, for business and social reasons.

But the rumors of removal were well founded. "The complication of moving the Kronprinzessin Cecilie is less military than legal," said the Boston *Transcript*. "The navigation problem is not insuperable. The course suggested by local pilots would be outside of the Cranberry Isles and Isle au Haut off Penobscot Bay, to Matinicus, passing either inside or outside of that rockpile; thence to Monhegan keeping preferably to eastward of it . . . and from Monhegan to Portland Head." When Captain Polack heard of this devious coastal voyage so gratuitously planned for him, he was appalled. The *Kronprinzessin*, he said, "is not a canoe."

The problem was not resolved until the captain himself went to Washington to confer with the Acting Secretary of the Navy, Franklin D. Roosevelt. There it was decided that the ship should be guided to Boston by destroyers. Dogged by British cruisers still patrolling offshore, the ship was towed to Boston for safekeeping in mid-November. There she was interned afloat in President Roads, just off Shirley Point and Deer Island, between the German ships *Köln* and *Ockenfels*. "Now that the Bar Harbor season is over," said a pundit, "perhaps the *Cecilie* would enjoy Palm Beach." But Boston would have to do. "You know," said Captain Polack to a group of local reporters as he pointed to his heart, "down here I am glad that I am in Boston. It was getting to be cold and lonesome at Bar Harbor."

Members of the *Cecilie*'s crew were allowed to go off now and then on fishing expeditions, and before long some of them were attending Boston night schools, taking books out of the Boston Public Library, and being otherwise swept up into the cultural climate of the Hub of the Universe. But when the United States entered the war, their ship was overhauled and converted into a troop transport. With most of her Teutonic features obliterated, the long, lean *Kronprinzessin Cecilie* became the good old S.S. *Mount Vernon*. Soon newspaper photographs would show her decks packed with doughboys grinning under the Stars and Stripes as they set off for the mud of France and the task of making the world safe for democracy. As for the urbane Captain Polack and his adaptable crew, who had so neatly fitted into American society, they were unceremoniously interned for the duration.

## QUEASY COME, QUEASY GO

Of all the scourges visited upon the traveller by sea—piracy, boredom, satyriasis, nymphomania, mildew, impressment into a foreign navy, scurvy, gluttony, claustrophobia, agoraphobia, hijacking, shanghaiing, sunstroke, malaria, paranoia, diarrhea, shipwreck, fire, ice, and fog—the one claiming the greatest number of victims and responsible for the deepest suffering was, by all odds, seasickness. "Gods! What a retrospect!" said one just back from its living grave. "It seems like an eternity of spasmodic suffering—talk of amputation! mental anxiety—chronic disease—why what is the whole catalogue of human ills compared to this attic salt!—this bilious dissolution—this sea-emetic?"

In spite of the witches' brews of preventives and curatives they carried on board with them, travellers escaped neither its green orchidaceous fever nor the warm soupiness of its embrace. In spite of prayers they offered day and night toward that end, very few travellers died of it. When seasickness overtook people who had survived amputation without anesthesia, suppuration without analgesia, asthmatic suffocation, gastric convulsions, and torture by the exquisite devices of imaginative aborigines, they recalled such miseries with the nostalgia and longing of old men remembering their youth. Anyone who has ever been seasick—classically seasick, as opposed to those mild forms of the malaise in which one is said to be "peaky," "squeamish" or "off his feed"—knows it is the only and ultimate sickness: the one living death of faculty and will that involves the whole man, individually and ontologically.

The end of this scourge of centuries of seagoing came abruptly and by accident, long after men had given up seriously looking for it. The place where the cure was discovered was the city of Baltimore; the year was 1947; the actual scene was the Allergy Clinic of the Johns Hopkins University and Hospital, on whose staff were Dr. Leslie N. Gay and Dr. Paul E. Carliner. Working as a team, these physicians were investigating the possible uses of a number of drugs in the relief of allergic conditions like rhinitis, urticaria, and hay fever. Among their drugs, forwarded to them for experiment by a pharmaceutical company in Chicago, was a synthetic antihistamine, $C_{17}H_{22}NO \cdot C_7H_6ClN_4O_2$, called dimenhydri-

*Mr. Slim is late, and takes a boat to the vessel.*

*He finds some difficulty in getting on board.*

*Out at sea. Squally. He goes to his state-room.*

*He enters his state-room in a hasty manner.*

*Mr. Slim in state-room—Position Number One.*

*Mr. Slim in state-room—Position Number Two.*

*In 1855 an unidentified artist—who obviously had sailed the great ocean at least once—drew this graphic picture strip.*

nate, and they had been giving it to a pregnant woman patient afflicted with hives. This patient, who had also suffered all of her life from carsickness, nevertheless had to make her visits to the clinic by streetcar. When it became evident that dimenhydrinate—or Dramamine, as it would soon be generally known—was curing her of hives, it also became evident that if she took a capsule of the drug before setting out on her cross-town journey, she got complete relief from the nausea that had always made her trolley rides a misery.

Alerted by her offhand report, the two doctors made their finding known to the United States Army—with the result that a troop transport engaged in ferrying military personnel and their families between Bremerhaven and New York was put at their disposal to carry out "Operation Seasickness." This ship was the thirteen-thousand-ton U.S.A.T. *General Ballou*, with a capacity of 1,376 passengers in austerity accommodations. She was scheduled to make a trip to Germany in November when, for the purposes of Drs. Gay and Carliner, the weather would be obligingly rough. To test the drug for both its preventive and curative properties, the physicians divided the 485 men chosen as subjects for the experiment into two groups. The first group, those chosen for testing Dramamine as a preventive, was then divided again, and approximately half of the men were given a Dramamine capsule of one hundred milligrams as the ship sailed out of New York Harbor. The second part of the subdivided group got a capsule containing only sugar. With the doctors alone in possession of the knowledge of who got what, similar capsules were ad-

ministered six hours later, then once before each meal, and before bedtime. One hundred and thirty-four men got Dramamine, and not one of them complained of nausea or vomiting while taking it. A hundred and twenty-three men got sugar capsules; of these, thirty-five became seasick within twelve hours of sailing. Drs. Gay and Carliner reported:

The corridors . . . were congested by sick men, so ill that they were unable to reach the latrines. The men who reached these areas were unable to return to their compartments and remained stretched out in semi-conscious condition on the floors until more seaworthy individuals managed to drag them to sick bay or back to their hammocks. The latrines became temporarily indescribably repulsive.

With one exception, all the afflicted men were brought back to normal by Dramamine within three hours.

*Feels uneasy, but thinks dinner will do him good.*

*After attempting dinner. Feels decidedly worse.*

*Feeling a little better, he proceeds on deck.*

*Walks forward. Big wave. Effect on Mr. Slim.*

*Odd feeling comes over him. Back to state-room.*

*Mr. Slim wonders if he is going to be sea-sick.*

*He called his rocky saga "Mr. Slim's Experience at Sea," and it was published, with the captions, in* Harper's Monthly.

*After a wretched bout of seasickness Sir Henry Bessemer, the British metallurgist, turned his ingenious attention to the age-old problem of* mal de mer. *What he came up with was a suspended saloon, shown in cross section above. In theory, those in or on it enjoy their voyage while others aboard clutch the sides. What happened to this wishful vision is described in the text.*

None of the men in the second group, the curative trial group, got any Dramamine at the beginning of the voyage. Fifteen of these became seasick; twelve got better at once when Dramamine was administered. In a whole crisscross schedule of tests and countertests on this voyage and a return voyage in December, on which a large number of the trial subjects were women, the doctors found that less than 2 per cent of the passengers who got Dramamine as a preventive measure were vulnerable to seasickness.

The way the drug worked, it turned out, was by offsetting "vestibular imbalance," the disturbance of the inner ear caused by prolonged unusual motion.

Drab in her Army gray, the *General Ballou* came back to New York bearing no visible sign that she was a ship of historical import, that she was worthy of a medal to be hung beside those memorializing the *Argo*, the *Golden Hind*, and the *Robert E. Lee*, or that the still-secret burden she carried was, to generations yet unborn, salvation on earth and a hope of heaven. Had Army regulations allowed it, the *General Ballou* should have run up a pennant imprinted with one word: *Eureka!*

A little pellet worth its weight in pitchblende had suddenly made obsolete all previous remedies for the prevention, cure, or endurance of *mal de mer*. These included the following: bismuth, soda, salol, opium, valerian, a combination of Beltafoline and soluble camphor, chloral, chloreton, "a little soup with cayenne," morphine with atropine, a slice of fat pork fried with garlic, "patience and a good walk on shore," hyoscine hydrobromide, a pint of sea water "in one gulp," phenacetin with caffeine, arrowroot and wine, sodium amytal, tomato sauce, mustard leaf, animal magnetism, trinitrin and cocaine, veronal, a spinal ice bag, luminal, small doses of tincture of iodine, mustard pickles, lemon and ginger, toasting the ear canals, caviar, cannabis indica, Worcestershire sauce, sodium nitrate, chewing gum, musk pills, dry toast, a belladonna plaster on the stomach, vinegar and water in sips, capsules of sodium phenobarbital.

"How pure and sweet the air would be at sea," said one lyrical observer, "if it were not for the repeated vomiting of bile, whose effluvia are extremely volatile and settle down at once in the curtains, floor, ceiling, paint, sofa and beds of the cabins." To cope with the effects of "ship's smell" and that disposition to immediate surrender it all but guaranteed, many people after 1908 depended upon a little pill that came, somewhat inappropriately, from Detroit. This was Mothersill's Seasick Remedy, certified "not to contain cocaine, morphine, opium, chloral, or any coal-tar products." Mothersill's, according to its makers, had received unqualified endorsements from such people as Bishop Taylor Smith, Lord Northcliffe, and hosts of "doctors, bankers and professional men, as well as leading clubwomen," all of whom had presumably been tranquillized and edified by the pill while "sailing the English Channel, Irish Sea and the Baltic." The cost of a box that would last the entire transatlantic voyage was one dollar. During World War I the firm's promotion reached out particularly to mothers of servicemen. "To Prevent Seasickness," read the advertisements, "and insure him a pleasant voyage, be sure to remember to put in his bag a package of Mothersill's Seasick Remedy."

Like every other remedy, Mothersill's for the most part worked only for those who thought it did. These were not apt to be among the serious sufferers, and many a box of the stuff lay barely touched beside the pale hands of the stricken.

Although later investigations would show decisively that psychogenic factors were of small account, the most time-honored method of treating

CONTINUED ON PAGE 98

BY JOHN SINGLETON COPLEY; COLLECTION OF MRS. HARRIET M. HARKINE

# MEN OF THE REVOLUTION–II

On October 10, 1775, Lieutenant General Thomas Gage took his last salute as commander in chief of His Majesty's forces in North America and the next day sailed for England aboard the transport *Pallas*. As he wound up nearly two decades of dedicated service in the American colonies, almost no one saw him off; and after his arrival in London a fellow officer wrote of him as a "poor wretch [who] is scarcely thought of, he is below contempt . . ." while other countrymen joked about the possibility of hanging him. For nearly half of those years in the colonies Gage had been the most powerful official on the continent; honest, honorable, a faithful servant of his king, he had given all he had to his task, only to be despised by the Americans and abandoned by the British.

It was ironic that Thomas Gage s colonial service should have begun and ended with two of the greatest disasters of British arms in North America—Braddock's defeat and the battle for Bunker Hill; yet in the twenty years between those bloody encounters the mood and circumstances in the colonies had altered forever, and forces totally beyond Gage's capacity to control had swept across the land like a whirlwind, catching him up, helpless, and wrecking his career in the process. (It may have occurred to him that his family, the Gages of Firle in Sussex, had an affinity for losing causes: his forebears had backed King John, Charles I, and James II.)

After attending Westminster, the famous public school, where his fellow scholars included a collection of names that would figure in the Revolution—Francis Bernard, John Burgoyne, George Germain, and two of the Howe brothers, George Augustus and Richard—Gage (as was then the custom) purchased a lieutenancy, fought the French in Flanders, and helped rout the Scottish clans at Culloden. In 1754 his regiment was posted to America, and in July, 1755, Gage was out in front with the advanced guard when the French and Indians struck General Edward Braddock's army. Wounded in the belly and the head, with several bullet holes in his coat, he nevertheless organized the rear guard for the retreat after Braddock was mortally wounded. He saw a thousand brave men killed that day, of fifteen hundred who went into action, yet Gage went back for more and was in Abercromby's suicidal attack on Montcalm at Fort Ticonderoga, where his friend Viscount Howe fell. Out of this wilderness experience came, in 1757, his proposal for a corps of disciplined irregulars—Gage's "chasseurs"—the first light-armed regiment in the British army. In 1760 Gage was made governor at Montreal; three years later he took command of British forces in North America.

Gage had demonstrated courage in battle, but he was not regarded as a brilliant commander; nevertheless, he had an aptitude for administration, and it was thought that his marriage to an American—the slender, ambitious Margaret Kemble—might be an asset. So in 1774, while Thomas Hutchinson, the governor of Massachu-setts, was home on leave, Gage was appointed to serve in his place in troubled Boston, retaining his rank as commander in chief. Good-natured, popular, with the face of a calm, even-tempered aristocrat, the conscientious Gage saw his duty and followed it, and could console himself that he had been patient and reasonable at every turn, in the face of exceptionally trying circumstances. One of his first acts in Boston was to put the unpopular Port Bill into effect—an event greeted by tolling bells, fasting, and public display of mourning—and every subsequent move he made on behalf of the king's ministers met with all the legal trickery and political chicanery known to the cantankerous, rebellious Yankees. He could have imposed martial law, but instead he permitted the town's residents almost complete freedom. He made no move to censor or suppress the scurrilous press; he allowed the rabble-rousers to hold their meetings; he did nothing to stop militiamen in outlying towns from drilling on village greens and collecting arms and ammunition. To set an example of justice to local authorities, he listened to complaints against drunken British soldiers and punished offenders with a flogging. All to no avail; for while the rebels called him a "monster" his own soldiers and the loyalists ridiculed him as "Tommy, the old woman."

Unhappily, Gage could not make policy; only London could do that. Again and again he wrote home, urging the government to take one clear course or another—either lop off the colonies "as a rotten limb from the empire, and leave them to themselves, or take effectual means to reduce them to lawfull authority." Leniency would not work, he knew; force and action might. Yet even when the government clamored for action they refused him the means with which to execute it. When on April 14, 1775, he received a dispatch ordering him to move decisively, to use force if necessary, and to arrest the principal rebels—at the risk of provoking hostilities —Gage ordered out the troops, with humiliating results at Lexington and Concord.

On June 17, when he was forced to move again, to capture the redoubt the rebels had erected in front of Bunker Hill, it was his final military act as commander, for the casualties of that frontal assault produced more than mourning in London; they incurred a bitter, unreasoning anger that demanded a scapegoat for defeat and national humiliation. And the scapegoat had to be the man who had pointed the finger of blame at his superiors for not giving him adequate support.

For a time after his return to England, Gage had hopes of obtaining an important post; there was even talk of giving him a new commission as commander in chief, but it came to nothing. Thomas Gage survived the war, living on until 1787, but the echo of his anguished cry after he learned the extent of his losses at Bunker Hill still rings in the ear: "*I wish this Cursed place was burned!*"
—*Richard M. Ketchum*

# Liberty and Disunion

*Three Centuries of Divorce, American Style*

Appearances may be deceiving, but marriage in the United States looks as if it is in trouble. More couples—primarily young—are living together without the formality of marriage, and more couples—somewhat older and sadder—are ending their existing marriages in the courts. Some see in this the onset of American morality's decline and fall. "Are we the last married generation?" asked columnist Harriet Van Horne in a 1969 essay. "Well, if we are, prepare for anarchy, chaos, and a breakdown in all the civilized amenities." True, those who dread the imminent death of marriage cannot find statistics of nonmarital pairings to support their fears. Such liaisons are not matters of legal record. But divorces are. And the records of them are coldly explicit. A Census Bureau report early in 1971 indicated that the number of divorced individuals in the population had risen some 33 per cent in the previous decade. While there were thirty-five divorced persons for every thousand married couples in 1960, there were forty-seven in 1970. The parade of couples to the courts to undo in repentance what they earlier wrought in mutual love is getting longer. That lengthened column, to some social critics, is evidence of a fresh disaster heaped by a permissive culture on venerable American institutions. They see a rising divorce rate as ominously in tune with an age of drugs, pornography, and flag burning.

Yet there is no new thing under the sun. In 1934 a Catholic publication lamented: "It is folly to say that the institution of marriage is in danger; the institution of marriage is gone." In 1927 a woman's magazine entitled an article: "Divorce for Every Marriage 1938 Prospect." In 1891 the *Nation* brooded over the increase in American divorces, a calamity that it ascribed to:

the general uneasiness and discontent with the existing constitution of society, to the decay in the belief in immortality and future punishment, to the great development of the means of travel and the migratory habits arising therefrom, to the enlarged consciousness of their rights . . . among women, and . . . the real increase of their independence due to new opportunities of self-support.

Four years earlier, in 1887, a New England clergyman had told an audience that in view of the rapidly increasing "evil of divorce" he doubted that there was "any considerable civilized people in the world . . . taking so great risks with the family as . . . these United States." And twenty years before that a church journal warned that divorce was on the march and a time was "rapidly approaching" when "the public sentiment on this point shall be almost wholly debauched."

Even earlier expressions of the same anxiety might be found. For divorce has long been a focus of debate in the United States, as in other nations inheriting the Judaeo-Christian tradition. On one hand stand those who see marital ruptures not merely in terms of individual pain and tragedy but as threats to marriage itself—a holy institution, the God-ordained source of the family, on which morality and civilization rest. In their eyes liberal divorce practices are dynamite for a responsible society.

On the other side are those who see in marriage simply an arrangement by which couples mate with tribal approval; a means for legitimizing children, sharing duties, and transmitting property and rank. Such "arrangements" may change from generation to generation with-

*By* BERNARD A. WEISBERGER

out threatening the peace of the community. And individuals whose attraction for each other has died with the passing years may separate—with provision for the care of their children—without a feeling of moral leprosy.

While such theoretical debates crackle, unsuccessfully married couples continue to separate in fact—often in fine disregard of the predictions made by prophets on both sides. How these men and women are then dealt with by the law creates the actual weave of divorce practice in any country. In the United States the basic tug between tight and loose divorce laws has been molded by unusual circumstances. Some aspects of American life have encouraged easy separation; others have built up an almost unequalled resistance to it.

American marriage bonds have been loosened by the diversity of backgrounds of an immigrant people and the migratory habits of the pioneers. In addition, marriage and divorce are matters reserved to the states, and the variety of jurisdictions offers many opportunities to the shopper for release from the marital tie. On the other hand, family-worship has been especially intense in the United States. This is because on the frontier the isolated family often *was* the indispensable carrier of civilized values. Furthermore, religion has played a large role in shaping American popular thought, and the voice of the preacher—whether Protestant circuit rider in the hinterlands or urban Catholic priest—has almost always been lifted to insist that what God hath joined, no man may put asunder.

England's American colonies inherited a complex pattern of divorce. In medieval days the fathers of the all-powerful Church decreed that the sacrament of marriage, once registered in heaven, could not be erased on earth. But even the canon law recognized that fate could create intolerable dilemmas. A spouse might go mad, disappear, or willfully and wickedly desert the marriage or even the Christian faith. In such cases ecclesiastical courts gave a kind of halfway divorce—*divortium a mensa et thoro*—from bed and board. The recipient was free of obligation to the offending partner but could not wed again. One marriage per lifetime was God's quota. But to this, too, there was an exception. The Church would grant *divortium a vinculo*—absolute divorce, with the privilege of remarriage—on the basis that the original marriage had never been valid. (In modern law this would be an annulment rather than a divorce.) Grounds for annulment could be the discovery of force or fraud in arranging the match, failure to have consummated the marriage, or the revelation that the partners were in some way related. Thus, a few kings and nobles with enough money and power, and a strong wish to discard a wife, could find canon lawyers who would discover some appropriate flaw in the distasteful match and cancel it.

But not invariably! Pope Clement VII refused to dissolve the marriage of King Henry VIII of England to Catherine of Aragon, and in the ensuing hurricane of royal wrath the Church of England was born.

The new church, as might well have been expected, at first looked rather tolerantly on divorce. But it insisted that only religious authorities could unite and divide couples in marriage, a point of view sharply challenged by the Puritan radicals of the seventeenth century. John Milton, the mighty bard of Puritanism, not only took the position that divorce was entirely the province of the state (in a pamphlet entitled *The Doctrine and Discipline of Divorce, Restored to the good of both Sexes from the Bondage of Canon Law and other Mistakes*), but he also suggested that the grounds be broadened. They should include any "contrariety of mind" hindering "the main benefits of conjugal society, which are solace and peace," because, the author of *Paradise Lost* declared, the true object of a Christian marriage was not "to grind in the mill of an undelighted and servile copulation."

When the Puritan Revolution in England ended with the restoration of the monarchy in 1660, the Anglican Church not only rejected this view but hardened its own divorce stand. It granted some bed-and-board divorces, but gave no annulments. The only way for an Englishman to get an absolute divorce was by a special act of Parliament, which would not even consider the case unless he already had an ecclesiastical bed-and-board separation. It was no wonder that between 1700 and 1850 only 229 wealthy, patient, and convincing British subjects achieved such final dissolutions.

The North American colonies felt the effects of this conflict in the mother country. Puritan Massachusetts sturdily insisted that marriage and divorce were civil matters, permitted only justices of the peace to perform marriages until 1692, and granted some forty divorces prior to that date (when a new charter cut down on Massachusetts' independence). Some of these divorces were given by the legislature, in imitation of Parliament presumably; some by a special court. The first one re-

ILLUSTRATED FOR AMERICAN HERITAGE BY MICHAEL RAMUS

corded was given in 1639 to the spouse of James Lux-
ford, for the compelling reason that he was proved to
have another living wife. Grounds for other divorces
granted later were adultery, desertion, impotence, incest,
and—a heartbreaking reality among a seafaring people
—long absence with presumption of death. Connecticut
and Rhode Island also dispensed legislative divorces
before the Revolution on similar grounds. Little Plymouth (where the Pilgrim Fathers landed) produced an
unusual divorce case when William Tubbs, carried
away by veneration for the Old Testament, tried to
divorce his wife in terms authorized in Deuteronomy
24:1. ("When a man hath taken a wife, and . . . she find
no favour in his eyes . . . then let him write her a bill of
divorcement, and give it in her hand, and send her out
of his house.") Tubbs handed Mrs. Tubbs such a "bill,"
prepared by himself and signed by witnesses. It was dis-
allowed by the authorities, but his case must have been
impressive, for they granted him a more judicially de-
fensible regular divorce.

In the southern colonies, however, where the influence
of the Church of England was strong, marriage remained
the monopoly of Anglican ministers. Divorces could only
be granted by bishops' courts; but since no such courts
sat in the colonies, there simply were no divorces.

Thus, from the beginning, America had more than
one set of rules for untying the marital knot. And, ironically, it was possible to do so in allegedly grim, Puritan
New England—but not in Virginia or the Carolinas,
supposedly the land of the pleasure-loving descendants
of the Cavaliers.

After the Revolution and the adoption of the Constitution each American state was a sovereign community so
far as matrimonial law was concerned. They proceeded
to use this exhilarating freedom in a variety of ways that
escape easy generalization. But certain patterns did
emerge. First of all, by 1860 almost every state had given
up the practice of legislative divorce and turned marital
separations over to the courts, under statutory guidelines.
Part of the reason was sheer self-defense. The amount of
committee time involved in investigating a divorce-bill
petition was prohibitive. But part was in the broad
stream of Jacksonian democratization. It was easier for
a man without "pull" to get his case onto a court docket
than a legislative calendar. One result of this development, however, was to freeze divorce into the American
judicial mold of adversary proceedings. Each divorce
was a dispute to be tried, with someone to be found
guilty of misconduct, instead of a no-fault investigation
into a human tragedy.

A second trend was toward eliminating bed-and-
board divorce. Though it lingered in a few states, most
legislators came to agree that a healthy young man or
woman legally separated from a spouse but forbidden to
remarry would sooner or later almost surely wind up
living with a partner, wedlock or no. In the words of a
Massachusetts legislative committee that successfully
urged abolition of the practice in 1870, it placed both
parties "in a situation where there is an irresistible temp-
tation to the commission of adultery." By then almost all
divorces granted in the United States were absolute.

*F*inally, there was a move toward broadening the
grounds for divorce, especially in New England and
the states of the rising West. Drunkenness, conviction of
felony, and cruelty were added to insanity, impotence,
adultery, and desertion as legitimate grounds for separation. The terms of the statutes became increasingly open
to broad construction. Connecticut in 1849 conceded the
possibility of divorce "for such misconduct as perma-
nently destroys the happiness of the petitioner." The
Nutmeg State already had a tradition of liberality. Its
legislature had granted a divorce to a man whose wife,
while sitting on another man's lap, commanded the husband to go home and take care of the children; and to a
wife whose breadwinner put dead chickens in her teapot
and wore his boots to bed. Ohio listed "gross neglect of
duty" among its causes. Indiana in 1824 adopted an
"omnibus clause," adding to all other stated grounds
"any other cause" deemed suitable by the judge. As a
result a substantial number of unhappy spouses began to
visit Indiana, swear out an affidavit of intended residence, and commence divorce actions. Illinois likewise
had rather easygoing practices. In 1867, for example,
Lieutenant Joseph H. Sylvester, of the United States
Army, was one of many divorce seekers in Chicago and
was awarded one on the substantial grounds of desertion by his wife. But later investigation revealed that
the affidavits testifying to her abandonment of him were

false; that she was notified of the proceeding against her by an advertisement published in the *Western Merchants' Prices Current* and by a bill posted on the door of the Chicago courtroom; and that in fact she knew nothing about her husband's intent until she received a copy of the decree by mail, in New York, where the lieutenant had left her. In 1852 Mormon Utah's territorial legislature empowered the courts to part couples who could not "live in peace and union together." Nevada, Wyoming, the Dakotas, and Oklahoma, both as territories and when admitted as states, also had broadly drawn divorce laws. What was more, because of their wandering populations of miners and cowhands, they generally required as little as six months to establish bona fide residence and the right to sue under those laws.

While liberalized divorce codes sometimes worked to the benefit of abused husbands, the general relaxation was part of the work of advancing feminism. Strangely enough, when the medieval Church originally made divorce difficult, it had the effect, intended or otherwise, of enhancing woman's status. A Christian wife was no heathen slave, to be thrown aside like a useless implement if she proved barren or if her man cast a possessive eye on some young potential concubine. But that was scarcely a problem for American wives in mid-nineteenth century. A more common situation was that of a woman hopelessly, helplessly tied to a drunken brute who was master of her property and her body, and whom she could not escape without becoming "guilty" of desertion, thus sacrificing her right to support and to custody of her children. Changing the law so as to empower judges to free such victims was a humanitarian act, part of the whole pre-Civil War drive toward lightening the burdens of the sick, the imprisoned, the insane, and the enslaved. Even male chauvinist lawmakers could not resist such rhetoric as that of Robert G. Ingersoll: "Is it possible that an infinitely wise and compassionate God insists that a helpless woman shall remain the wife of a cruel wretch? Can this add to the joy of Paradise, or . . . keep one harp in tune?"

But the march toward a Zion of easy divorce was not an unchecked triumphal procession. Most divorces were still granted on conventional grounds, like that given to John Pyle of Kentucky in 1819 from Lucinda Woodward, whom he espoused in the faith "that she was a virtuous and chaste woman," only to find later that she was "sometime advanced in a state of pregnancy with another man." Moreover, there were holdouts; there was impassioned debate; and as the century ended, there was a definite pendulum swing of reaction. New York, for example, repeatedly defeated efforts to amend its 1787 law, which allowed no grounds for divorce save proven adultery, while South Carolina was even more adamant and made no provision at all for divorce. South Carolina was traditionally a bastion of conservatism (as late as 1860 it still had its legislature choosing the Presidential electors). In New York the political combinations opposing divorce-law changes always held a majority.

*I*n the general clamor of argument over what made the good society, marriage and separation were debated with increasing fervor in the middle third of the century. There were anti-Christian spokesmen like Henry James, Sr. (father of the novelist and the psychologist), who wrote in a newspaper debate: "Jesus Christ may be an excellent practical authority for your and my private conscience, but he should not be writing the laws of social union." There were rampant feminist individualists like Victoria Woodhull, who advocated that the state keep its hands entirely off the relationships between men and women and who, when taunted with advocating free love, shot back: "Yes, I am a Free Lover. I have an inalienable constitutional, and natural right to love whom I may, to love as *long* or as *short* a period as I can, *to change that love every day* if I please." There were freethinking political liberals like Indiana's Robert Dale Owen, veteran of the utopian community of New Harmony founded by his philanthropist father. Owen pointed out that the existing law allowed a husband to assault and rape his wife nightly with impunity, provided that he supported her—and that this made her a particularly harshly exploited prostitute.

Opposing such ideas were marital conservatives like the New York *Tribune*'s editor Horace Greeley (a violent reformer of other institutions), who sputtered in 1852 that liberalizing the laws of divorce would "result in a general profligacy and corruption such as this country has never known, and few of our people can adequately imagine." It would create a world in which "libertines would resort to marriage as a cloak for lecherous de-

CONTINUED ON PAGE 100

# American Gothic

By WAYNE ANDREWS

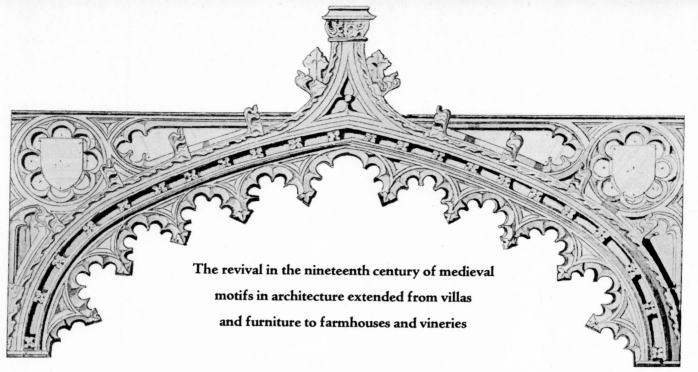

**The revival in the nineteenth century of medieval
motifs in architecture extended from villas
and furniture to farmhouses and vineries**

Many of the visitors who admire the classic calm of Monticello would be startled if they knew of the original intentions of Thomas Jefferson. In 1771, after he had begun work on the estate, he seriously contemplated building a battlemented tower on a neighboring mountain; and he also planned, though he did not actually erect, "a small Gothic temple of antique appearance" for the graves of his family and retainers. As usual, the master of Monticello was ahead of the times. Some sixty years would pass before such things were fashionable in America.

The notion that the Gothic Revival was *fashionable* would, incidentally, have greatly distressed the leaders of the movement in the United States. They were men of principle, and there was nothing frivolous in their arguments. They labored, in the thirty-odd years between Jackson's first term and Lincoln's, in the hope that America would one day acquire a fine medieval look. They were disappointed, as we know, but they tried hard. They saw to it that many of our prisons were Gothic; they built a Gothic capitol in Louisiana; they could point, in Graniteville, South Carolina, to a completely Gothic mill town; and before they grew old, they had the satisfaction of knowing that every self-respecting suburb in the

land had a castle or at least a cottage in the Gothic style. Finally, when it came to ecclesiastical architecture, they won a victory that no one could dispute. Even in our day there are those who believe that a non-Gothic church is the height of eccentricity, very like a wedding without the march from *Lohengrin.*

A certain frivolity did mark the beginning of the movement in eighteenth-century England. There *might* have been a Gothic Revival without Horace Walpole, but it would not have been half so entertaining. "I am going to build a little Gothic castle at Strawberry Hill," he wrote Sir Horace Mann, the British minister at Florence, in 1750. "If you can pick me up any fragments of old painted glass, arms, or anything, I shall be excessively obliged to you. I can't say I remember any such things in Italy; but out of old chateaus, I imagine, one might get it cheap, if there is any." No one could ignore the amusements of a Walpole, and by 1764, when he wrote *The Castle of Otranto,* the first of the Gothic novels, the craze for Gothic villas could not have been halted even by an act of Parliament.

Of Walpole's imitators, the most splendid was William Beckford, the gorgeously rich son of the Lord Mayor of London. In 1796 he began the building of Fonthill Abbey, the

great tower of which rose 276 feet. The tower was none too solid; it eventually crashed into a noble ruin, but this was after Beckford had disposed of his abbey to gunpowder merchant John Farquhar for £300,000.

Americans with money to spend could not resist the charm of Strawberry Hill and Fonthill, and by 1799 the first Gothic villa had been built in the United States. This was Sedgely, the respectable cottage of merchant William Crammond in Philadelphia. Sedgely has disappeared, but its architect, Benjamin Henry Latrobe, will not be forgotten, for he was the man most responsible for the design of the United States Capitol.

Although Daniel Wadsworth, the cultivated son of an Army commissary general, Jeremiah Wadsworth, insisted on Gothic trim for the frame house he set down on top of a hill near Avon, Connecticut, about 1800, and although that highly respectable Philadelphia fishing club The Castle of the State in Schuylkill made its headquarters Gothic as early as 1812, the new style did not become a national phenomenon until shortly after Andrew Jackson entered the White House in 1829. Before the architects could perform, the critics had to seduce.

The first of our Gothic prophets was Congressman Gulian Crommelin

*It was Horace Walpole, the originator of the fashionable literary genre known as the Gothic novel, who also inspired the craze for villas in the medieval style when he built Strawberry Hill on the bank of the river Thames in the 1750's. This detail is from a painting by John Henry Muntz, a Swiss who was employed by Walpole.*

Verplanck of New York, who was as devoted to the progress of the fine arts as he was to the formation of a sound tariff policy. When Verplanck was invited to lecture before the American Academy of Fine Arts in 1824, he could not resist expressing his disgust for the work of Samuel McIntire, the Massachusetts wood-carver-architect who built many of the notable houses of Salem, and the other practitioners of what we call the Federal style. He was frankly bored, said Verplanck, by "that corruption of the Roman, or rather Palladian architecture, which delights in great profusion of unmeaning ornament, in piling order upon order, in multitudes of small and useless windows, columns, and mean and unnecessary pilasters."

It was time, the congressman hinted, for America to set out on the Gothic quest. Verplanck wondered if even the temples of Greece were as inspiring as the Gothic cathedrals with "their peculiar and deeply interesting associations which, I know not how, throw back the architectural remains of the Middle Ages to a much remoter antiquity in the imagination than those of Rome and Athens."

This was a telling argument. Verplanck had introduced the fourth dimension, time itself, as an essential element of architecture, and the day would come when even a prosaic stockbroker, radiant at the thought of retreating to the Tudor era at eventide, would decide on a Gothic house for his family. Perhaps if Verplanck had not had the tariff problem constantly on his mind, he might have become the leader of the Gothic crusade. As it was, the distinction passed to the young Andrew Jackson Downing, a landscape gardener from Newburgh, New York, who had an entire magazine, *The Horticulturist*, in

which to promote his views.

Downing was a worthy standard-bearer, earnest in preaching the Gothic, impatient with the Grecian heresy. The Greek Revival, which had been imported from England by Latrobe in the year in which he built Sedgely, was, to tell the truth, much more popular than the Gothic. To Downing this was more than regrettable; it was inexcusable. "The Greek temple disease has passed its crisis," he hopefully reported in 1846. "The people have survived it."

Like all great prophets Downing kept his admirers at a distance. One of them wrote, "He had a natural fondness for the highest circles of society—a fondness as deeply founded as his love of the best possible fruits." Downing appreciated the magnificent ring the Queen of Denmark forwarded in homage to his writings, but his gratitude was muted, since he was "marked by the easy elegance and perfect savoir-faire which would have adorned the Escorial." Except for a pile of letters on his desk he tolerated no sign of labor in his Gothic home.

Labor he did, however. But for his efforts and those of William Cullen Bryant, Central Park might not have been saved for New Yorkers a century ago (not that it is out of danger yet). Downing had the good sense to insist that the beauties of nature were not too fine for the average citizen. He also had the intelligence—or prescience—to talk like Frank Lloyd Wright when discussing the nature of materials. "When we employ stone as a building material, let it be clearly expressed," he urged. "When we employ wood, there should be no less frankness in avowing the material."

For Downing, architecture must fit the client, if not the other way around: "To find a really original man living in an original . . . house is as satisfactory as to find an eagle's nest built on the top of a mountain crag, while to find a pretentious, shallow man in such an habitation, is no better than to find the jackdaw in the eagle's nest."

Downing made plain that he was not writing for the timid. "There is something wonderfully captivating in the idea of a battlemented castle, even to an apparently modest man, who thus shows to the world his unsuspected vein of personal ambition," he declared. "But *unless there be something of the castle in the man*, it is very likely, if it be like a real castle to dwarf him to the stature of a mouse."

Here was a message—*i.e.*, no turrets for the Walter Mittys of the nineteenth century—that any architect could understand. No one, however, was more alert in tracking down the clients that Downing dreamed of than the architect A. J. (Alexander Jackson) Davis, who had the privilege of contributing a number of illustrations to Downing's handbooks besides being puffed in the pages of *The Horticulturist*. Although Davis was guilty of more than one design in the Grecian manner—the capitol of North Carolina was perhaps the most famous—these were lapses that could be forgiven. He was, as everyone knew, a Goth at heart.

Davis was a brilliant draftsman, and in the informal, irregular plans of many of his Gothic castles he delivered so fierce an attack on the formal planning America had inherited from the eighteenth century that he has every right to be considered one of the founders of modern architecture. Unlike any modern architect that we have heard of, he entered the profession through a trap door.

All his life, his diaries reveal, Davis was a conscientious reader of Gothic novels. As a boy, enchanted with the unhappy heroines of Mrs. Ann Radcliffe's tales, he lived for the hours in which he could steal to the attic and sketch the mountainous retreats where those ladies were imprisoned. For days he would puzzle over the plans of "some ancient castle of romance, arranging the trap-doors, subterraneous passages and draw-

*The Delineation of Fonthill and its Abbey*, BY JOHN RUTTER, 1823

bridges." It was only when an older brother urged him that he would pry open a book of history or attempt to solve the riddle that was mathematics.

The son of the editor-publisher of a Congregationalist review in New York, Davis may have been a worry to his parents, for he gave every indication of going on the stage. While setting type for his brother, who ran a newspaper in Alexandria, Virginia, he joined a "philodramatic" society composed—so he told an aunt—"of the most respectable young men" and more than once appeared behind the footlights. But he also created the sets for *Bertram*, a Gothic drama, and later, after returning to New York, he realized that his mission was to be an artist. Toying with that old sketching tool, a camera obscura, he suddenly began "designing streets in Venice, conjecturing the fashions of gondolas, and planning interiors for churches, palaces and prisons." Told by Rembrandt Peale that he was meant to be an architect, he got his first training in the studio of John Trumbull, an artist who believed he had mastered the funda-

*The most noteworthy English imitation of the style set by Strawberry Hill was cathedrallike Fonthill Abbey, designed for William Beckford, the son of a Lord Mayor of London, by the architect James Wyatt in 1796. Its size was awe-inspiring, as the dimensions indicate. The great hall, below, was 120 feet high; the octagonal tower rose 276 feet. Despite its look of solidity, the tower collapsed in 1825 because of a weak foundation, and the rest was later razed.*

*For a Victorian tryst, a Gothic gazebo*

*An entrance gate of wood and ironwork*
*Villas and Cottages,* BY CALVERT VAUX, 1857

*The vinery on a Hudson River estate*

mentals of the architectural profession in his afternoons off from painting the American Revolution.

In 1828, when Davis was barely twenty-five, he earned the opportunity of a lifetime. Ithiel Town, a prosperous bridge builder and architect, invited him to be his partner. When Town went off on a grand tour of England and the Continent in 1829, Davis was left in charge of the office. Six years later, when Town retired, the younger man was already in the midst of the most successful career of any romantic designer. Indeed he had so many commissions that he could afford to ask Town back into the firm in 1842 and 1843. And when his good friend Downing perished in the sinking of the Hudson River steamboat *Henry Clay* in 1852, Davis was so well established that he could face the future without a qualm.

Davis may have suffered only one major disappointment: he was not given the chance to design a castle for Jay Gould. This was most unfortunate, since the lord of the Erie Railroad was a dedicated student of the Gothic. The perfection of Gould's taste was evident in the map of Albany County that he drew up and peddled as a young man; along its borders were portrayed a number of Gothic villas, and any architect should have realized that the young surveyor had the makings of a serious client.

In the end Gould paid his tribute to Davis by buying the greatest of all his castles, Lyndhurst, at Tarrytown. Originally planned in 1838 for William Paulding, the brother of Van Buren's Secretary of the Navy, this was too ambitious a house in the opinion of diarist Philip Hone, mayor of New York in 1825–26. Unmoved by its graceful asymmetry and complex masses, Hone decided that it was "an immense edifice of white or gray marble, resembling a baronial castle, or rather a Gothic monastery with towers, turrets, and trellises;

minarets, mosaics, and mouse holes; archways, armories, and air holes; peaked windows and pinnacled roofs, and many other fantastic too tedious to enumerate, the whole constituting an edifice of gigantic size, with no room in it; great cost and little comfort, which, if I mistake not, will one of these days be designated as 'Paulding's Folly.'"

Mayor Hone may be entitled to his opinion, but no lover of the Gothic Revival could possibly agree. The plan, in all of its irregularity, provided not only for comfort but for a really generous scale of living. Fortunately, Lyndhurst's attributes can now be shared by the well-to-do and commoner alike; after several years of litigation over the will of Gould's daughter, Anna, Duchesse de Talleyrand-Périgord, who died in 1961, the great mansion came under the aegis of the National Trust for Historic Preservation and is now open to the public. [See "The Realms of Gould," in the April, 1970, AMERICAN HERITAGE.]

However, many other brave designs by Davis in the Gothic manner have been the victims of neglect, greed, or impudence. Perhaps it was logical (though scarcely admirable) of New York University to destroy the great marble halls of the old campus on Washington Square; perhaps it was excusable for a real-estate speculator to pull down the House of Mansions, an imposing crenellated row of houses—this time of brick surfaced with plaster—that stretched from the southeast corner of Fifth Avenue and Forty-second Street; perhaps it was inevitable for some other developer to demolish Murray Hill, the lovely brick villa at Fifth Avenue and Thirty-seventh Street once owned by stockbroker W. H. Coventry Waddell; perhaps it was just as inevitable that the inviting villa of C. B. Sedgwick in Syracuse, New York, would be demolished after being used to house an advertising agency.

No such plea could be advanced in the case of the destruction of Walnut Wood, the villa at Bridgeport, Connecticut, of the leather dealer H. K. Harral. When the last coat of plaster was applied to the façade, it was obvious that Davis had almost reached the heights of Lyndhurst. The plan at least was nearly as commodious. With all its Gothic furnishings Walnut Wood was lovingly preserved by the last owner, Archer C. Wheeler, who was so public spirited that he deeded the mansion to the city. However, Mr. Wheeler was scarcely buried when the house was torn down in 1958. The public protest was immense, but futile.

Searchers after the Gothic in America will be reassured to learn that there are a number of examples by Davis beyond the grasp of the demolishers of this world. The original clubhouse of the New York Yacht Club, which stood first in Hoboken and then at Glen Cove, Long Island, has been recently removed to the security of the grounds of the Marine Historical Association

at Mystic, Connecticut. A whimsical frame cottage with ornament dripping from the eaves, this was an ideal place in which to toast the winners of the America's Cup. We should be happy, too, that the fine old office building of the nursery firm of Ellwanger & Barry is still standing in Rochester, New York. Quite unlike any office building that we know of, it could be taken for the gate lodge of a Tudor castle. Safe, too, are a couple of lyrical frame cottages: that in Rhinebeck, New York, of the local banker Henry Delamater, and that in New Bedford, Massachusetts, of mill owner W. J. Rotch. Finally, the grim but noble stones of the Wadsworth Atheneum in Hartford are in no apparent danger and, indeed, were unobtrusively wedded to a new four-story annex in the late 1960's.

Nor has Davis been discarded by the South. The towering, crenellated brick-and-stone buildings on the campus of Virginia Military Institute at Lexington, ravaged in the Civil War, were promptly rebuilt as

*The first Gothic villa to be built in the United States was Sedgely, the home of the Philadelphia merchant William Crammond. It was designed in 1799 by Benjamin Henry Latrobe, chief designer of the Capitol in Washington, D. C. This water color is by David J. Kennedy, the gifted artist whose views of Philadelphia life will be displayed in our December issue. Anything could be Gothic, including the bark-framed tool shed with shingled roof, below.*

*Villas and Cottages*

31

*The pointed arch was the leitmotif of the
Gothic Revival. Together with other deco-
rative frills it was carefully carved in wood
to adorn the furnishings inside great houses.
Arches even adorn the sewing-machine stand
at left. Below it, from A. Pugin's definitive*
Gothic Furniture *(1827), are a sofa and
footstool that call to mind Italy and the Le-
vant. Large, intertwining leaves—another
familiar Gothic theme—are the chief feature
of the bed. Other fifteenth-century touches
grace Pugin's whist table, bottom left, and
the tall wood-burning stove of 1820 directly
below. On the opposite page, top to bottom,
are an entranceway to a Gothic home, the
Grand Lodge Room of the New Masonic
Hall in Philadelphia dedicated in 1855, and
a perspective view of a graceful staircase.*

Davis intended—possibly because
v.m.i. cadets had served under Stone-
wall Jackson. And Belmead, the
spectacular plaster-finished castle of
General Philip St. George Cocke
in Powhatan County, Virginia, has
been saved from the wreckers by
conversion into a Roman Catholic
school for Negroes.

No one, incidentally, was more devoted to Davis than Cocke. It was he
who insisted that Davis must be in
charge of the building program at
v.m.i. He once wrote the architect,
"If I was autocrat or even emperor
(like Louis-Napoleon in France), I
should delight with your aid to build
up the waste places, repair delapida-
tion . . . and beautify the goodly and
glorious heritage of our Rip Van
Winkle people. But recollecting that
I am but a democratic unit, I must
limit and control these flights of
fancy."

Another devoted client was the
wholesale druggist Llewellyn Haskell, whose passion for romantic
scenery led him to found Llewellyn
Park at West Orange, New Jersey—
perhaps the most sensible real-estate
development in American history.
Davis was the creator of the ambitious stone gate lodge that still de-
fends the domain. Although only one
frame Gothic cottage in the park today stands undefiled to proclaim the
architect's intentions, he will always
be associated with the ravines therein.
"We thank Mr. Davis, the Michel
Angelo of his time, for what he has
done for us," exclaimed a critic in
1859. "No other man could have
combined nature and art."

The "Michel Angelo" of the hour
was not, of course, the only outstand-
ing practitioner in the Gothic style.
Churches, which he rarely attempted,
were the particular province of Richard Upjohn and James Renwick, Jr.,
two architects who could scarcely be
overlooked in the most cursory sur-
vey, especially when the weight of
the Gothic legacy in church building
is given its due.

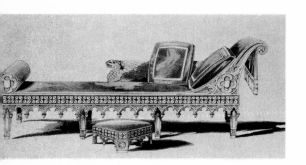

"Distress," Upjohn noted in his journal on the way from his native England in 1829, "is not a proper subject for merriment or topic for invective." This high-minded Anglican, who was a wretchedly worried man in his first years in the New World, apparently had no time for the Gothic novels that were Davis' evening indulgence. Although he fashioned a sturdy stone Gothic castle for Robert H. Gardiner, of Gardiner, Maine, and a particularly charming frame Gothic cottage at Newport for Gardiner's son-in-law from Savannah, he vastly preferred ecclesiastical commissions. To him they meant peace on earth.

Describing his ambition, Upjohn declared, "The object is not to surprise with novelties in church architecture, but to make what is to be made truly ecclesiastical . . . such as will fix the attention of persons, and make them respond in heart and spirit to the opening invocation: 'The Lord is in His Holy Temple; let all

GRAND LODGE, F. & A. M. OF PENNSYLVANIA

---

## HOUSES IN AMERICAN HISTORY

*The American Heritage History of Notable American Houses* is just off the press. In this 384-page, copiously and colorfully illustrated book, the history of life in America is told in terms of the houses Americans have planned, built, and lived in— from the caves and hovels of the first arrivals to the sophisticated inventions of today and tomorrow. A companion volume, *The American Heritage Guide to Historic Houses*, provides an exhaustive list of homes, from Maine to Hawaii, that are open to the public. The books are available as a set at $19.90. Correspondence should be sent to American Heritage Subscription Office, 383 West Center Street, Marion, Ohio 43302.

---

the earth keep silence.' " This was his frame of mind when he conceived Trinity Church, New York, the greatest of all his churches and one of the rarely challenged monuments of the Gothic Revival. Perhaps this serious-minded man should be forgiven for his doubts concerning denominations other than the Church of England. He once designed a Presbyterian church —but with misgivings. A rival reported that although he did it "conscientiously," he believed that "Presbyterians were not entitled to architecture."

Upjohn's rival James Renwick, Jr. was a talented man, even if not so loyal to principle. He was the only American architect to keep two steam yachts, one for fishing off the Florida coast, the other for cruises in more distant waters. He insisted on the high style becoming an artist, a frame of mind aptly illustrated in the alarming castle he designed in 1851 for C. T. Longstreet of Syracuse, a merchant who had the wit to send the first ready-made suits to the West Coast after the gold rush. Built of stone, the castle looked like a fortress in the moonlight. It was annihilated by Syracuse University following World War II, after many years of service housing the School of Journalism.

Although Renwick was the creator of St. Patrick's Cathedral, New York, his finest achievement was Grace Church, farther downtown. Completed in 1846, when the architect was only twenty-eight, Grace made a favorable impression even on Philip Hone. As Hone correctly noted, "This is to be the fashionable church, and already its aisles are filled (especially on Sundays after the morning services in other churches) with gay parties of ladies in feathers and mousseline-de-laine dresses, and dandies with moustaches and high-heeled boots; the lofty arches resound with astute criticisms upon *Gothic architecture* from fair ladies who have had the advantage of foreign

TEXT CONTINUES ON PAGE 97
ILLUSTRATIONS CONTINUE OVERLEAF

*A. J. Davis' most magnificent mansion, Lyndhurst, at Tarrytown, New York, was built in 1838 for William Paulding. Later, after*

*Davis enlarged the house, Jay Gould became its owner. One of the few Gothic Revival homes extant, Lyndhurst is open to the public.*

Davis achieved an amazing variety of visual effects in the use of Gothic themes, as demonstrated in the designs on this page, both of which feature crenellated towers and window arches. The water color above, made in 1848, is of Walnut Wood, the house in Bridgeport, Connecticut, he built for H. K. Harral. Later bought by a family named Wheeler, the house was razed by Bridge-port in 1958, an act of artistic vandalism bitterly protested by preservation groups. Below is the House of Mansions, designed in 1858. A series of eleven houses, all attached, it once graced Fifth Avenue at Forty-second Street in New York. Opposite is the house Davis built for his mother in Newark, New Jersey, in 1850, also no longer standing. He even planned the details of its landscaping.

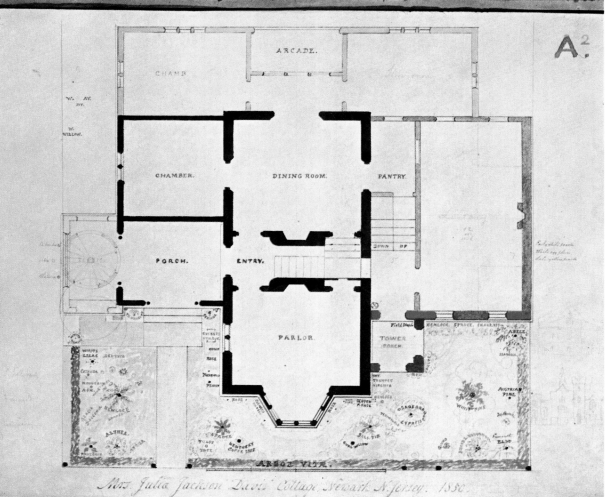

ARCADE.

CHAMB

CHAMBER. DINING ROOM. PANTRY.

PORCH. ENTRY.

DOWN DF

PARLOR. TOWER PORCH.

ARBOR VITÆ.

*Mrs. Julia Jackson Davis' Cottage, Newark N. Jersey. 1850.*

*Foreboding in the best tradition of the Gothic novel is Davis' rendition of the home for John J. Herrick, built in 1855, that once*

*stood in Tarrytown, New York. Because of the profusion of such villas in the area, the style became known as Hudson River Gothic.*

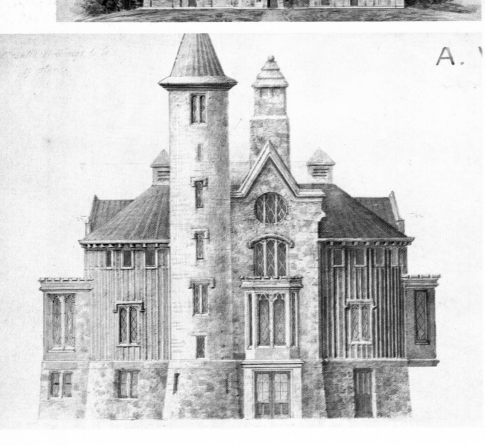

*Alger. D.*

*No. 5.*

A. V.

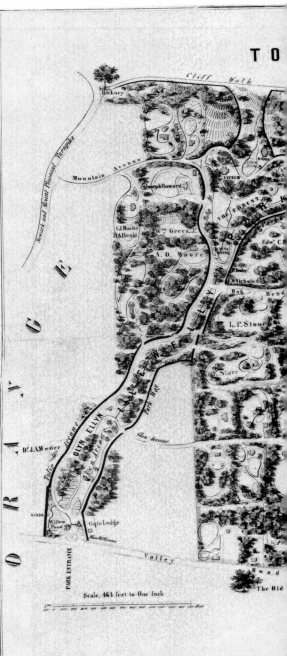

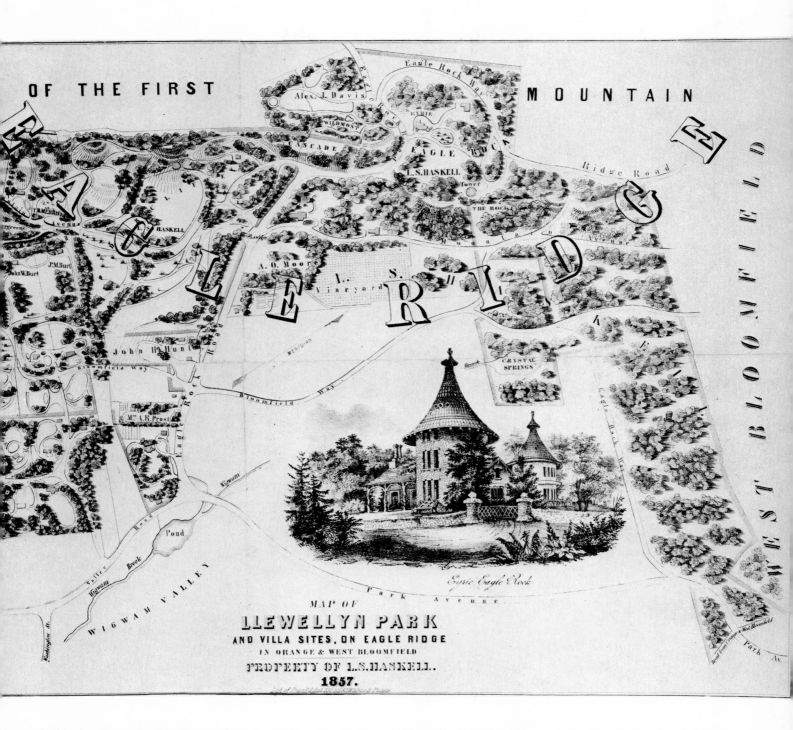

MAP OF
# LLEWELLYN PARK
### AND VILLA SITES, ON EAGLE RIDGE
IN ORANGE & WEST BLOOMFIELD
PROPERTY OF L.S.HASKELL.
**1857.**

*Besides Lyndhurst, Davis' other great legacy was Llewellyn Park, nestled in the foothills of the Orange Mountains in New Jersey. Only one original cottage and the Gate House to the park still stand today, but the landscape design remains, and the streets still wind grace-fully amid the luxurious estates. The development was founded in 1857 by Llewellyn S. Haskell, whose own conical Eyrie Eagle Rock is featured above on the map he distributed to prospective buyers. Its tower points to Haskell's estate. To its left is Davis' own place, Wildmont, shown in full stateliness on the opposite page, bottom. Above it are two other houses from the park, the cottage of E. W. Nichols (top) and the castellated Anderson residence. The Gate House that survives looks much like Haskell's Eyrie, torn down in 1923.*

# RURAL RESIDENCES, ETC.

CONSISTING OF DESIGNS,

## ORIGINAL AND SELECTED,

FOR

## COTTAGES, FARM-HOUSES, VILLAS, AND VILLAGE CHURCHES:

WITH BRIEF

EXPLANATIONS, ESTIMATES, AND A SPECIFICATION

OF

MATERIALS, CONSTRUCTION, ETC.

———————

BY ALEXANDER JACKSON DAVIS, ESQ.,

AND OTHER ARCHITECTS.

PUBLISHED UNDER THE SUPERINTENDENCE OF SEVERAL GENTLEMEN, WITH A VIEW TO THE
IMPROVEMENT OF AMERICAN COUNTRY ARCHITECTURE.

NEW YORK:

TO BE HAD OF THE ARCHITECT, AT THE NEW YORK UNIVERSITY,
AND OF THE BOOKSELLERS GENERALLY, THROUGHOUT THE UNITED STATES.

MDCCCXXXVII.

To promote his architectural designs, Davis published in *1837* a bookful of specifications and costs for a wide choice of buildings. One of the "*several gentlemen*" who assisted in the publication was Robert Donaldson, whose villa on the Hudson River, *Blithewood,* appears below. It follows the English Collegiate style, "*suited to scenery of a picturesque character.*" Davis offered to repeat the building in wood for $8,000. Its gate house, above, was in the so-called rustic cottage style, and it cost $1,200.

Davis' versatility as an architect skilled in many styles is seen in the mélange of buildings from his **Rural Residences** on these pages. At left, graced by a Norman tower, is his Village School House, which he said should have a situation "such as to produce in the minds of the pupils, in after life, pleasing recollections of the spot where they received the rudiments of their education." Below, a Greek temple was the inspiration for what Davis called a Log, or American, House. The Gothic spirit for which he was noted is evident in his Farmer's House, above on the opposite page, and in the Village Church below it. The church, he noted, is designed "in the English Decorated, or Third Style of Pointed Architecture, vulgarly called Gothic." Davis built one of these lovely edifices, Christ Church at Belleville, New Jersey, for "about $9,000." It no longer stands.

# GOTHIC GONE COMMERCIAL—AND GODLY

*Brought to the city, Gothic Revival architecture lent an air of Old World grandeur to otherwise humdrum façades and interiors. The show rooms of the marble works in Philadelphia, at left below, even had arched niches with statues. Lithographer W. H. Rease perceived another Gothic fillip in the horsecar windows. Close by was Charles Oakford's Model Hat Store, whose interior we show about 1854. Richard P. Morgan, Jr.'s design for an elevated railway in Manhattan, an airy series of pointed arches, looks too fragile to support a train. Morgan estimated it would cost $400,000 per mile to build. No one took him up on it. A pity.*

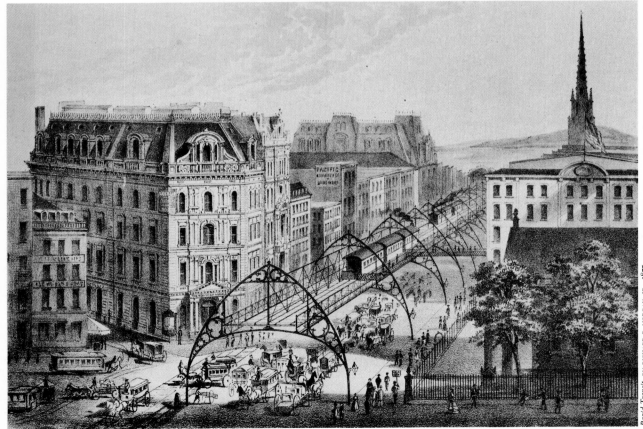

*Rapid Transit,* BY RICHARD P. MORGAN, JR., 1875

*The Floating Church of the Redeemer, a Gothic wonder that rested on two 100-ton barges, was used by Philadelphia's Churchmen's Missionary Association for Seamen to bring God nearer to where He was needed most. The edifice burned down in 1868 after being moved to a more conventional foundation on land.*

# Miss Eleanor Roosevelt

*"She is such a funny child, so old-fashioned, that
we always call her 'Granny,'" her mother said.
Cousin Franklin felt otherwise*

*By* KENNETH S. DAVIS

By no strange quirk of fate, no unlikely chance or mysterious destiny, were Eleanor and Franklin Roosevelt brought together in casual acquaintanceship. Even had they been wholly without ties of blood and family tradition, unsharing of the same family name and distant ancestry, the strangeness would have been in their *not* meeting as they pursued their highly mobile physical lives within that small social world, close-knit and rigidly exclusive, which both of them inhabited.

And in actual fact they did meet for the first time when she was only two years old. On a day in 1886 her parents came to Hyde Park as houseguests of James and Sara, Franklin's parents, bringing her with them— a plain-visaged, remarkably solemn little girl whom her mother called Granny and her father Little Nell and who stood around in doorways with her finger in her mouth, excessively shy, silently withdrawn, until four-year-old Franklin set about en-

tertaining her. And himself. He (her distant cousin, her father's godson, her future husband) took her into the nursery to play "horsey"; she sat astride his back as he romped joyously around the room on his hands and knees. . . . She herself had no later recollection of this, of course; she would learn of it from her mother-in-law.

But she remembered meeting him again when she was in her early teens and was forced to attend dances at which she was miserable while he, to all outward appearances, was perfectly at ease and thoroughly enjoyed himself. One such occasion was, for her, especially memorable. It was during the Christmas holidays, the only time of the year when she was permitted to see boys her own age. All the other guests knew one another well: she alone was a stranger, an outsider, with nothing about her that could (she felt) attract anyone's favorable attention, much less actively interest a boy. Already she was

taller than most grown women; and since she was, by her grandmother's decree, inappropriately dressed in a little-girl's skirt that reached barely to her knees, her height became an exaggeration, a kind of vertical elongation of her natural awkwardness. She was rigid with embarrassment. She knew herself to be a poor dancer —felt herself more graceless on the dance floor than perhaps she was, in actual truth. And so she watched in helpless envy as other girls danced, one after another, and flirted, too, with her handsome Cousin Franklin, an urbane Harvard man who was evidently admired by all. Then he spied her. He came to her. He asked her to dance with him, and asked, moreover, as if he really wanted her to! She was almost tearfully grateful to him.

The next encounter, as far as either of them could later recall, was on a New York Central train. She was then eighteen and had just returned from schooling in Europe.

OPPOSITE: *Miss Eleanor Roosevelt at fifteen (1899)*

She was on her way from New York City to Tivoli on the Hudson to spend the summer in her grandmother's house when he, sauntering through the day coach in which she sat, recognized her and took her back to talk to his mother, who, of course, despite the shortness of the ride, occupied a Pullman seat. She would never forget how formidably beautiful his mother had seemed to her that day. James Roosevelt had died only six months before. Sara (Eleanor's "Cousin Sallie") was still in mourning, clad all in black, with a heavy veil that fell from hat to feet, and the somberness of her attire somehow accentuated the brilliance of her eyes and the classic purity of her features. She appeared at least a decade younger than her actual years.

A few months later Eleanor Roosevelt was introduced to New York society at an Assembly Ball where she knew only two unmarried men and suffered again agonies of humiliation over her lack of popularity and, as she profoundly believed, the means of ever achieving it. She fled the ballroom as early in the evening as she possibly could. But not long afterward her Aunt Tissie and Uncle Stanley (Mr. and Mrs. Stanley Mortimer) gave a large party for her— theatre, late supper at Sherry's, followed by dancing—that went very well, and from then on the "season" proceeded for her more smoothly, less unhappily, through a crowded sequence of luncheons, teas, dinners, suppers, dances where, inevitably, she met her fifth cousin Franklin from time to time. She continued to meet him the following autumn after her Grandmother Hall had decided not to open the old Hall family brownstone on West Thirty-seventh Street that year, 1903 (the cost of doing so was too great), but instead to permit Eleanor to live with her Cousin Susie and Susie's husband, Mr. and Mrs. Henry Parish, in the city. She and Franklin became good friends that fall, then better

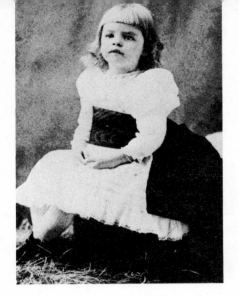

*Eleanor at three: a typical "Granny" pose*
FRANKLIN D. ROOSEVELT LIBRARY

friends as the holidays came and passed.

All of which, as regards their relationship, was in general outline predictable.

The event emergent from it, however—the intimacy that grew up, that ripened into love—seemed to most observers no fruit of the inevitable. Indeed, there was about it, if not an actual strangeness or mystery, at least an improbability, an unlikelihood that bred surprise. Few could have foreseen it, even with a vision armed by the most intimate knowledge of their very different characters, temperaments, upbringings; and these few emphatically could not have included Sara Delano Roosevelt. Franklin's mother was more than surprised; she was initially shocked. And when the shock wore off she was deeply hurt, with a hurt that contained a sense of outrage and insult.

First the shock.

It came to her in the great white house her Grandfather Warren Delano had built in Fairhaven, the house now legally owned by all the Delano brothers and sisters but actually managed, along with the trust fund that accompanied it, by Sara's elder brother, Warren III. The Delano clan had gathered there for Thanksgiving, 1903. And perhaps it was on Thanksgiving Day itself in a room

redolent of the turkeys that roasted in the kitchen—possibly a room containing mementos of the old China trade and, upon one wall, the coat of arms of Jehan de Lannoy, Knight of the Golden Fleece—perhaps it was then and there that he told her, as tactfully as possible, after a considerable verbal preparation, that he had fallen in love with Eleanor Roosevelt, had proposed marriage to her, had been accepted.

His mother was visibly staggered. She could not at first believe her ears. Her handsome son "had never been in any sense a ladies man," according to her recorded belief. "I don't believe I remember ever hearing him talk about girls . . ." she later wrote. Certainly he had shown no slightest romantic interest in any girl. Yet here he was, a college student who had cast his first ballot less than three weeks before, who had yet to earn a dollar of his own or decide definitely upon a career—here he was, not seeking her advice, much less her permission, but simply flatly informing her, as of an accomplished and irrevocable fact, that he was going to be married! And to Eleanor Roosevelt! Of the girl's suitability in terms of family and social standing there could be no question, though her immediate family situation might well raise certain doubts: she was a Roosevelt, after all, and a niece of the President of the United States. Moreover, she was a sweet thing, rather pathetically so, eager to please and gratifyingly grateful for every kindness shown her. But she seemed not at all the kind of girl who would seriously attract Franklin, being quite easily classifiable, in the metaphorical botany of the day, as both wallflower and (potentially at least) clinging vine. She was certainly not beautiful. Her large lustrous eyes were truly lovely, and she had a good figure and complexion; but all this was offset by her protruding teeth and slightly receding chin and by the self-conscious awkwardness she often displayed. She shared few if any of Franklin's active interests. She was not good at winter sports, she was a poor sailor, she couldn't swim, she played neither tennis nor golf, and she had no special interest in nature nor any at all in collecting. She seemed old for her age (she was only nineteen), and in unattractive ways, being excessively tense and earnest, as well as timid and retiring, with little evident force of mind or charm of personality. What, then, did Franklin see in her?

And how could he have arrived at his decision, through a process that must have extended through months of increasingly frequent meetings and growing intimacy, without his mother's having had the slightest inkling of what was going on?

To her there seemed but one explanation of her surprise. Her son had been *deliberately* secretive, had taken pains to exclude her from knowledge of the most important development in his life thus far; and she could not but feel this as a derogatory and even a contemptuous commentary upon herself and her relationship (she had believed it to be an almost perfect rapport) with her son. It was as if she were being cast aside —her love spurned, her authority flouted, her wisdom denied, her loneliness assured. And her first response, after the shock wore off, seems to have been a more or less calculated play for sympathy, an expression of hurt that was like a sword aimed at the tender heart and filial conscience of her son, at the faint heart and puritanical self-denial of Eleanor.

From Fairhaven Sara went with Franklin to New York City. He brought Eleanor there from 8 East Seventy-sixth Street, the home of the Henry Parishes, to his mother's apartment, where, on Tuesday, December 1, "I had a long talk with the dear child," as Sara wrote in her di-

ary. On the following day Eleanor wrote to her "Dearest Cousin Sallie" (one suspects she pondered the salutation) at Hyde Park: "I must . . . thank you for being so good to me yesterday. I know just how you feel & how hard it must be, but I do so want you to learn to love me a little. You must know that I will always try to do what you wish for I have grown to love you very dearly during the last summer. [She had spent much time visiting at Hyde Park and Campobello that summer.] It is impossible for me to tell you how I feel toward Franklin. I can only say that my one great wish is always to prove worthy of him." Thus she indicated the price she was willing (or believed she was willing) to pay for her acceptance, sounding a note of abjectness that boded ill for her development of an independent individuality vis-à-vis either the imperious Sara or Sara's son. There was nothing abject about the letter Franklin wrote from Cambridge two days later: "Dearest Mama—I know what pain I must have caused you and you know I wouldn't do it if I really could have helped it—mais tu sais, me voila! That's all that could be said—I know my mind, have known it for a long time, and know that I could never think otherwise: Result: I am the happiest man just now in the world; likewise the luckiest—" To which he added blandishment: "And for you, dear Mummy, you know that nothing can ever change what we have always been and will always be to each other—only now you have two children to love & to love you—and Eleanor as you know will always be a daughter to you in every way—"

So she, the mother, changed tactics. Already it had been agreed that this engagement should be kept secret for the time being. Now she set about prolonging the "time being" into an indefinite but distant future, her grounds being that both Franklin and Eleanor were too young to know

what they really wanted, much less to assume the grave responsibilities of marriage and children. She pointed out that her own father had not married until he was thirty-three, by which time he was "a man who had made a name and a place for himself, who had something to offer a woman." What did Franklin have to offer that was truly his own? His inheritance from his father had been a relatively modest one: he must depend upon his mother's largess or his own earned income if he were to maintain the standard of living to which he and Eleanor were accustomed. And how was he to earn an income? He planned, tentatively and with no enthusiasm, to enter law school the following autumn. He could not complete his course work there and pass his bar examinations for nearly two years after that. Surely it was the part of wisdom to delay marriage until he was actually a bona fide member of some well-established law firm.

Nor was this all.

To the tactics of delay she added those of diversion. The real purpose of a proffered Caribbean cruise in early 1904 was to enforce Franklin's separation from Eleanor for many crucial weeks during which he, with his friend Lathrop Brown, would be totally immersed in strange new scenes, new excitements, and would emerge with new perspectives whereby (she hoped) his mind would be changed. Both her son and Eleanor were fully aware of this purpose. Eleanor resented it. She resented not only Cousin Sallie's offer of the cruise, with all that it implied, but also (perhaps more so) Franklin's acceptance of it. And she may well have communicated some sense of her resentment to him as he bade her good-bye in New York. At any rate he began the cruise in a grumpy mood ("F. is tired and blue," wrote his mother in her diary on the day they sailed) and did not recover his spirits until they were well out to sea.

As for Eleanor, if she watched him go with bitterness in her heart, if she was condemned now to a period of anxiety colored with despair, the experience was certainly not new to her. The tall gawky adolescent girl who had been so miserable at Christmas holiday parties in New York had grown up out of a miserably unhappy childhood.

She had no later remembrance of her mother's calling her Granny during her first visit to Hyde Park when she was only two, but she did remember all her life other occasions when her mother did so, and

*Just after the death of her mother in 1892, Eleanor posed with her father, holding baby brother Hall, and brother Elliott.*
BOTH: CULVER PICTURES

wounded her by doing it. She was the oldest child of Elliott and Anna Hall Roosevelt. She had two brothers: Elliott ("Ellie"), a couple of years younger than she, and Hall ("Josh"), nearly six years younger. And she never forgot how, when the three children were with their mother for a children's hour in the late afternoons, she suffered always a sense of alienation from the others. Josh, the baby, cuddled and caressed, sat happily on his mother's lap. Ellie, adoring his mother and obviously adored by her in turn, responded with laughter and gay chatter to his mother's advances. But the little girl felt herself excluded from this circle of love by "a curious barrier," as she later recorded. They were together; she was alone. She knew that her mother not only did not love her as

she did the others but actually found her unattractive in appearance and personality—knew, or sensed, that the emotion she aroused in her mother was a mingling of pity with disappointment, irritation, embarrassment, even shame—and knew, too, that it was partly out of a sense of guilt for feeling this way that her mother "made a great effort" on her behalf. And all this came to a focus of pain on days when her mother, entertaining visitors, saw her hesitating in the doorway, a forbidden finger in her mouth, and called to her in a voice that had an edge of exasperation: "Come in, Granny!" Often then the mother would turn to her visitors and say: "She is such a funny child, so old-fashioned, that we always call her 'Granny.'" Eleanor on such occasions "wanted to sink through the floor in shame."

The hurt was all the greater because she so admired her mother for the beauty and charm that were recognized (the little girl early learned) throughout New York society, a society her mother deemed Important. She longed for her mother's affection, or at least approval. She never received it. On the contrary, "I was always disgracing my mother."

Often she did so through a "habit of lying" rooted in her fears, her insecurities, her craving for acceptance. When she was five she was taken with brother Ellie to Europe by her parents, toured Italy with them, and was then placed in a French convent for several months while her father entered a sanitarium and her mother took a house in Neuilly, just outside Paris. She was put in the convent because her mother, expecting a baby (Josh was born early that summer), sought to protect her innocence against all knowledge of how children come into the world. She was terribly lonely there. She knew herself to be plain-faced and ill-mannered, and she would have been isolated in any case from the other little

girls by differences of language and religion. One day a girl there swallowed a penny and thereby made herself the focus of excited attention, arousing Eleanor's envy; and so, sometime later, she, Eleanor, went to the sisters saying that she, too, had swallowed a penny. She hadn't, of course. The sisters knew she hadn't. But she persisted in saying she had until her mother was sent for and took her home in disgrace. She acquired thus a label, an identity, by which her mother and (consequently) she herself were horrified: she was a liar! And she was confirmed in this identity by being found out in other lies as the years of childhood passed—about eating sugar and candy, for instance, when these were forbidden her by the family doctor.

The long angry scoldings she received for these offenses were far more dreadful to her than "swift punishment of any kind," so dreadful that her fear of them sometimes encouraged the evil they were meant to correct. "I could cheerfully lie any time to escape a scolding, whereas if I had known that I would simply be put to bed or be spanked I probably would have told the truth," she later remembered.

Almost the only loving contact she ever had with her mother was when Anna took to bed with a sick headache. These headaches were frequent and severe; and when they came the little girl would sit at the head of the bed stroking her mother's throbbing temples and forehead and neck for hours on end. She was grateful for being allowed to sit there, but at the core of her gratitude was the happy knowledge that her mother's willingness was not merely permissive. She could feel her love flowing out through her caressing hands into her mother's beautiful head, alleviating pain, bringing peace; she knew that her presence was, for a change, truly welcome. She was being useful. And in her childhood the rare "feeling that I was useful was perhaps the greatest joy I experienced."

Her mother, alas, had good reason to suffer nervous headaches: her marriage to Elliott Roosevelt, so joyously begun, grew tragic, and she was being subjected to intolerable strains. Elliott had been a remarkably attractive young man, much more so than his older brother Theodore. He was good-looking, spontaneous, sensitive, gay, and highly intelligent. But he had also rather more than his share of the character defects that so often accompany great charm. He and Anna had not long been married when there came a recurrence of the mysterious illness, a failure of will and nerve, that had forced Elliott's withdrawal from prep school when he was in his teens. It began shortly after the birth of his first son. It was triggered evidently by a riding accident in which his leg was broken. The break was a very bad one and so poorly set that later, after months of acute pain, the leg had to be rebroken and reset—an event that Eleanor, though a very little girl at the time, never forgot. "... I sensed that this was a terrible ordeal," she wrote a half century later, "and when he went hobbling out on crutches to the waiting doctors, I was dissolved in tears and sobbed my heart out for hours." Amid this prolonged physical anguish he began to drink heavily.

There began then, for him, a long, hard, and ultimately futile "fight for ... health [he never completely recovered physically from the effects of his accident] and power of self-control," a first step of which was his entrance into the sanitarium in France while his wife awaited the birth of Hall in Neuilly. He made no very satisfactory response to the medical treatment given him there, evidently, for his daughter remembered that when he came to the Neuilly house

on temporary release from the sanitarium, he caused his wife and his sister "a great deal of anxiety," that he remained in the sanitarium when his family sailed for home many weeks after Hall's birth, and that finally "his brother, Theodore, had to go and get him . . ." He continued to drink. No "cure" brought more than temporary relief. And in a time and place when the label for such as he was not the neutral one of "alcoholic" but the opprobrious one of "drunkard," he was a disgrace to his wife and family—so great a one

*Anna Hall Roosevelt, 1892*

that his highly religious wife could not bear it. He was sent away, or went away, to a little town in Virginia, while his wife and children lived more and more with Eleanor's Grandmother Hall; they stayed in Elliott's New York house during the winter months but spent most of the warm seasons at Oak Terrace in Tivoli.

The effect of all this upon the little girl, Eleanor, was devastating. Her father's love for her, joined to hers for him ("he . . . was the love of my life"), constituted the one bright warm flame in the otherwise chilly gloom of her childhood. When he called her Little Nell it was not as her mother called her Granny but, instead, as one speaks a term of endearment, of delight in one's beloved; and she knew this long before he explained that Little Nell was a char-

acter in Dickens' *Old Curiosity Shop*, a book he made her read when she was old enough. He never made fun of her, save in a teasing way that further indicated his love for her, his pride in her. With him she was always "perfectly happy." And when, in France, she was caught lying about swallowing the penny, her father, who was himself in disgrace (she sensed this from the tears and words and gloomy looks of her mother and her Auntie Bye), "was the only person who did not treat me as a criminal!" When he first went away, to Abingdon, Virginia, she was desolate. She couldn't understand why he had left her. She desperately needed the reassurance he gave her in a letter he wrote from his exile, saying: "My darling little Nell . . . Because father is not with you is not because he doesn't love you. For I love you tenderly and dearly—and maybe soon I'll come back well and strong and we will have good times together, like we used to have."

Alas, he never did come back "well and strong" to live with his family. Perhaps he was making definite progress toward that happy end when suddenly death struck down his beautiful young wife.

In early December, 1892, Anna Hall Roosevelt fell ill of diphtheria. Her little daughter was taken to stay with Mrs. Parish, her Cousin Susie. And it was there that Eleanor was told, on the seventh of that month, that her mother was dead. She knew something horrible had happened, but she could not feel that she personally had suffered a great loss; and such sorrow as she did feel was more than overcome by the joy she felt when told that her father would soon come to Mrs. Parish's to see her. He did come, after a while. He took her driving, up Madison Avenue and over to Central Park. He was as charming, as kind and loving to her as ever. But she soon realized that this was, for him, a time of absolute tragedy. He was deemed incompetent—no doubt he deemed himself incompetent—to make a home for his children. They were taken instead to live with their Grandmother Hall, in the brownstone on West Thirty-seventh Street. And Eleanor never forgot his sadness as, in the gloomy library of that house, he (dressed all in black) took her in his arms and spoke of his bereavement and of how he had now only his children, of whom the two boys were too young for him to really talk to, so that it must be she and he together. Always they must remain close, even though physically separated, until someday they would live together, travel together, do all manner of interesting things together.

Thereafter she lived on the hope, the promise thus given her. She needed a bright future to look forward to, for her actual present life in her grandmother's house was, if anything, more gloomy and unsettling, more prolific of psychological insecurities, than life with her mother had been. Two uncles, Vallie and Eddie, two aunts, Pussie and Maude, still lived in their (and her mother's) childhood home. They were out of control, having grown up without guidelines after their father's early death, without imposed standards of conduct. Their various storms and clashes of willful temperament, especially Vallie's and Pussie's, made the atmosphere of the house on Thirty-seventh Street and Oak Terrace in Tivoli anything but peaceful. And Grandmother Hall's reaction to this, as far as her grandchildren were concerned, was a determination that they "should have the discipline her own children had lacked," so that ". . . we were brought up on the principle that 'no' was easier to say than 'yes,'" as Eleanor later recalled. Moreover, she was in the care of a French maid, Madelaine, who scolded her and pulled her hair and of whom she was, for reasons she never quite understood, desperately afraid.

Hence her yearning, her vital need for her father.

He came to the New York house for a second sorrowful visit in that same winter of his wife's death. Ellie and Josh had come down with scarlet fever, the latter recovering with no permanent ill-effects; but Ellie, in his weakened condition, had caught diphtheria and quickly died. Eleanor, who was never seriously ill—she was practically never ill at all—was taken again to the Parishes, where she was quarantined.

During the next two years her father came but seldom to the Hall home, for brief visits only, generally without prior notice. Yet his daughter, who seems always to have subconsciously waited for him, never failed to sense his presence from the instant he opened the front door, and she flew into his arms, sliding down the banisters if she was upstairs. Despite his prolonged absence he "dominated all this period" of his daughter's life. He took a great interest in her education, which her mother had been inclined to neglect, and she learned many things just to please him—most of *Hiawatha* by heart, for instance. She was by her own account a great physical coward but was frequently able to overcome her timidity when she was with him, because he so disapproved of it. He gave her puppies, and a pony, and loaded her down with presents at Christmastime and on her birthday. He wrote her often; and as she read his letters, she shared joyously in what she believed to be his life, which was apparently full of little children, and fox terriers, and horses. She lived with him in a dream world.

Then he died.

On August 14, 1894, shortly before her tenth birthday, her Aunt Maude and Aunt Pussie came to her and told her that her father was dead. She wept for him: she was swept by a storm of tears and wept

for a long time in her bed that night, before an exhausted sleep overcame her; but in her deepest self she would not, could not accept the fact that he was forever gone from her, that she would never see him again, and when she awoke next morning she "began . . . living in my dream world as usual." She was helped to do so by her grandmother's decision that neither she nor Josh should go to the funeral, for this meant that she had "no tangible thing to make death real to me." She knew in her mind that her father was dead, yet could not or would not *feel* that he was, so that for a long time "I lived with him more closely, probably, than I had when he was alive."

A thicker gloom than she had known before, less often interrupted by beams of light, closed down around her.

For instance, while her father lived, a bright spot of almost every week in the city for her had been a Saturday visit with her father's aunt, Mrs. James King Gracie (Auntie Gracie), sister of her Grandmother Roosevelt. Auntie Gracie was a warm, vibrant person, "much beloved by her great-nephews and nieces," of whom Alice Roosevelt and Teddy Robinson were generally with her at the same time as Eleanor was. The three Roosevelt cousins had much fun together and had learned things, too, for Auntie Gracie talked to them by the hour, often about plantation life in the South, where she and her sister had been raised; took them sightseeing in the afternoons and to such educative entertainments as Mrs. Jorley's waxworks; and sometimes took them to visit the Orthopaedic Hospital that Grandfather Roosevelt had helped to found and where the sight of "innumerable little children in casts and splints" aroused in Eleanor a great pity and desire to help alleviate the pain and suffering in the world. Always, the little girl had looked forward to these rich Saturdays. Then—abruptly, with no reason given—they were forbidden her by her grandmother.

Indeed, Grandmother Hall discouraged all contacts between her grandchildren and the Roosevelts. Perhaps she resented as well as disapproved of the family whose son, in his weakness, had brought such great sorrow upon her daughter. Perhaps she feared that her grandchildren, if they were too much exposed to their lively and dynamic Roosevelt relatives, would escape or rebel against the rigid control she was determined to maintain over them. Whatever the reason, Eleanor was permitted no more than a couple of visits to the home of her Aunt Edith and Uncle Ted at Sagamore Hill, Oyster Bay, Long Island—visits that stood out so sharply, vividly from the dreary monotony of her average childhood days that she always afterward remembered them in detail. She remembered her terror as she jumped off a dock into the ocean, upon her Uncle Ted's orders, despite her inability to swim (he insisted that this was the way to learn, but it didn't work). She remembered her almost equivalent terror when Uncle Ted lined her up with the other children atop a high, steep, sandy bluff and had them all run pell-mell down it to a beach, most of them falling on the way and then rolling to the bottom—an exercise she rather enjoyed after she had learned that a fall wouldn't hurt her. Terrified or not, she always felt, when she was with Uncle Ted, that she was alive. Truly alive. And she remembered with unalloyed pleasure being chased by Uncle Ted through haystacks, being read to by him in the house (poetry, for the most part), and going with him and the others on a camping trip during which he "taught us many a valuable lesson"—especially "that camping was a good way to find out people's characters"; the selfish would reveal their selfishness by shirking their share of the work of the camp and by seeking for themselves the best food, the best bed.

On West Thirty-seventh Street and at Tivoli she had almost no companionship with children her own age. She was much alone, and in her solitude she became an omnivorous reader, going often into wood or field with a book, in the summertime, to read for hours, and reading in bed (though this was forbidden) in the mornings before she arose. She had occasional good times with her uncles and aunts, especially with Uncle Vallie, who was gay and charming with her, and Aunt Pussie, who was an accomplished pianist, much interested in the theatre (she took Eleanor to see Duse), and permitted her niece to wait upon her, run errands for her, to the little girl's great delight.

But these good times were more than balanced by tempestuous times with her uncles and aunts, especially Pussie. For Pussie had what was called an "artistic temperament," meaning that she was highly emotional and had a meager sense of responsibility. Once she took Eleanor and Eleanor's governess to Nantucket, where, after a few days, she casually abandoned them, going off without telling them where she was heading or leaving them any money to pay for lodging or transportation home. The frantic governess had finally to obtain the needed money from Grandmother Hall. Such treatment, coupled with her grandmother's inveterate habit of saying No ("I built up the defense of saying I did not want things in order to forestall her refusals and keep down my disappointments"), did nothing to build up the little girl's self-confidence or sense of security. Small wonder that she entered adolescence as a shy, gawky creature who, at parties, was made painfully aware that she was "different from all the other girls," and in ways that were unattractive.

Not until she was fifteen and was enrolled in a school in England conducted by a remarkable Frenchwoman, Mlle. Souvestre, did she

again receive any such affectionate concern for her essential self, any such sympathetic understanding, as she had received from her father. The school was run on lines little if any less austere than those at Groton, where Franklin Roosevelt was enrolled; yet Eleanor thrived in this environment. She felt that she was set free of the past, with all its sins and terrors and repressions, and could begin anew. The result was that "for . . . the first time in all my life . . . all my fears left me," including those born of that "physical cowardice" of which she had formerly been ashamed. Required to play some game or other, she chose field hockey, the roughest of all, and managed to make the first team ("I think that day was one of the proudest . . . of my life"), suffering proportionately as many hard knocks and bruises as Franklin had suffered in Groton football. She was accepted by the other girls, was even popular with them, and made friendships that would last a lifetime.

But it was Mlle. Souvestre herself who gave the greatest boost to her morale. Mlle. Souvestre, in late middle age, had an executive temperament, a strong character, a hard, prosaic mind—and her pedagogical techniques, her overall influence upon the girls in her school, were in several respects similar to those of Endicott Peabody upon the boys at Groton. Every night, for example, the girls were assembled in the library to bid good-night, one by one, to the headmistress, whose "eagle eye," on such occasions, "penetrated right through to your backbone and . . . took in everything about you." Therefore it meant an immense amount to Eleanor that she should soon become, and know that she had become, one of Mlle. Souvestre's favorites. She was abruptly cured of her "habit of lying," know-

*Summer, 1904: F.D.R. and Eleanor dally at Campobello during their engagement.*
BROWN BROTHERS

ing that she had nothing to fear from truth telling so long as she conformed to clearly defined rules and regulations. She was improved in her dress and manners by Mlle. Souvestre's expressed tastes in these things. And she was "shocked . . . into thinking" by Mlle. Souvestre's unorthodox views on politics and religion. In politics the headmistress was a liberal; in religion she was an atheist and frankly said so: she was convinced that religion in general was designed for, and needed by, the weak only. The effect of this last was especially salutary upon Eleanor, who had been so strictly raised in so gloomily religious a home. She was under the beneficent influence of this remarkable teacher for three school terms, plus many weeks of vacation during which she and Mlle. Souvestre toured the Continent together.

But even during the years when this influence was being actively exerted, it was interrupted and counteracted by the influence upon her of her mother's family.

She went home for the summer following her second term in the school. Her Aunt Pussie had come to Europe, and with Pussie she shared a cabin back across the Atlantic. The

boat was a slow one; the voyage seemed interminable. For Pussie, who had a penchant for violently unhappy love affairs, had just reached the end of one and spent most of each night sobbing and threatening suicide, adding an almost intolerable anxiety to the seasickness from which Eleanor always suffered. Nor did she escape Pussie's "artistic temperament"—wherein selfishness and self-indulgence were now streaked with a mean cruelty—during the weeks that followed. She went to stay for much of the summer with Mrs. Parish at Northeast Harbor on Mount Desert Island, Maine. Pussie stayed with a Ludlow aunt of hers nearby. And one day when she was furious with her adolescent niece for some reason, the ineffable Pussie plunged and twisted into the girl's sensitive soul the cruellest knife of words that could possibly have been devised at that time, in those circumstances. First she did her best to destroy the personal confidence, the mild self-esteem which the girl had begun to develop in Europe: she said flatly that Eleanor must never expect to have beaux, as the Hall women had always had, because she, Eleanor, was the ugly duckling of the family. Then she proceeded to tell the girl about Elliott Roosevelt's last years, giving his daughter ugly facts that had theretofore been carefully kept from her. Eleanor was cut almost to death; Mrs. Parish could do little to assuage the pain, much less to heal wounds that remained open and bleeding when the girl returned to her Grandmother Hall's house. As for Grandmother Hall, she was too much preoccupied with her oldest son Vallie to give any sympathetic attention to Eleanor, for Vallie, after a brief period of exemplary young manhood, "was now beginning to sow his wild oats" with a vengeance. He was well on his way toward chronic alcoholism, if he was not already there.

It was thus with relief that Eleanor, with Aunt Pussie, moved not

long afterward into the West Thirty-seventh Street house, leaving her Uncle Vallie with her grandmother at Tivoli—a move that somewhat decreased her misery. But life was far from peaceful and happy with Pussie, whose "love affairs were becoming more serious" and who sometimes "shut herself into her room" for days at a time, "refusing to eat and spending hours weeping." Eleanor finally made attempts to discover the precise nature of her sorrowful aunt's troubles but was unable to do so; she was confronted instead, and in consequence, "with many situations that I was totally unprepared to handle." Nor did she wholly escape her Uncle Vallie. Every now and then, despite her grandmother's desperate efforts to keep him in the country, he came roaring down the Hudson to the city house "for one purpose and one alone . . . to go on a real spree" (as if his average drunkenness were not "real" enough), requiring of Eleanor (because Pussie was too preoccupied with herself to cope with the difficulties he imposed) a full exercise of strengths and braveries and managerial skills she had not theretofore known she possessed. And Uncle Vallie was not the only sad, insoluble family problem she had to face at this time. Her Uncle Eddie was now married but proved himself wholly incapable of handling this responsibility or any other; he, too, had become an alcoholic.

Thus Eleanor, in the season of her "coming out" and of an acquaintance with her cousin Franklin Roosevelt that grew toward intimacy, supped often on horrors in her most private life and, at some cost in terms of spontaneity and resilience, was strengthened by them in terms of essential character. She recognized the horrors to be the result of a complete loss of the power of self-control. She was determined, therefore, never to lose her own, but instead to increase it, building upon a habit of self-denial that had been forcibly impressed upon her from her earliest years. She developed what later appeared to her as an "exaggerated idea of the importance of keeping all of one's desires under complete subjugation."

In general her experience had made of her by this time a curiously mingled mind and personality. In many respects she was innocent and unworldly to a degree remarkable for one of her age and circumstances. She had, as she later recalled, "painfully high ideals and a tremendous sense of duty entirely unrelieved by any sense of humor." She knew virtually nothing about how most people earn their living or about the handling of money: not until she was nineteen and living with the Parishes did she learn, from Mr. Parish, how to keep books and avoid expenditures in excess of income. She knew nothing, through personal experience, about sexual and other intimate relationships between man and woman: she was always rigorously chaperoned when with a man, had never been kissed by one, and would have been insulted by the attempt of any man to kiss her or give her an expensive present who had not first proposed marriage and been accepted. But as regards other matters of which most women of her class were wholly ignorant—matters pertaining to what was then generally called the seamy side of life—she knew a great deal, thanks to her long and frequently bitter experiences with Vallie and Pussie, plus the tragedy of her father.

By the quality of both her innocence and her sophistication, coupled with the sense she continued to have of herself as hopelessly unattractive and socially maladroit, she was unfitted for "success" in that formal society in which she was willynilly involved and which, because of family teaching and example, she continued to deem important. She

did her duty as she and the Hall family saw it. She went to the required dinners and dances night after night. But she greatly preferred and actually enjoyed the informal studio parties given by a famous woman painter to whom she was introduced by a bachelor friend much older than she; and she became truly engaged by other activities having nothing to do with society as such. The Junior League was then a new organization through which privileged girls undertook to earn their privileges to some degree by charitable and social work of various kinds. Eleanor became an active member. With Jean Reid, daughter of the Whitelaw Reids, she taught calisthenics and "fancy dancing" to slum children in the Rivington Street Settlement House. She also became active in the Consumers' League, going with an experienced older woman to investigate (and be shocked by) working conditions of girls in garment factories and department stores.

And so she came to the autumn of 1903, to a memorable weekend spent in Groton, where she visited her young brother Hall and was visited by Franklin Roosevelt, who, then and there, after some weeks of increasingly ardent courtship, asked her to marry him.

She had evidently by then got over the astonishment, the incredulity with which, in view of her expressed assessment of herself, she must have received his first intimations of a serious romantic interest in her. Perhaps she was even able by then to see herself a little through his eyes and realize (though she contradicted this in later recollection) that she was, if no beauty, by no means without physical, sexual attractiveness. For though awkward when tense, and often tense (because timid) in social situations, she had the tall slender grace of a young willow when at ease and could not but feel, when her lover looked deep into her eyes, that this was so. She knew that her eyes were actually

*"Cousin Sallie," Franklin's mother, makes a point or two for an attentive Eleanor.*
FRANKLIN D. ROOSEVELT LIBRARY

beautiful, knew that Franklin had been attracted to her in response to no conscious effort on her part (she had been passive, receptive, and permissive only within the iron bounds of the formal conventions that had so strictly governed her upbringing), knew that he and she shared certain fundamental sympathies and antipathies—and from this knowledge had been born a warm sense of inner security greater than any she had known before.

It was so great, in fact, that his asking her to marry him seemed to her "an entirely natural thing." He was so absolutely sure of his feelings, so sure of what he wanted! She herself, it would appear, was not so sure. When she returned to the Parishes after that Groton weekend she "asked Cousin Susie whether she thought I cared enough," a question that would hardly have occurred to her had she been deeply, passionately in love. And she herself later confessed that though she "solemnly answered 'yes'" when asked by her grandmother if she was "really in love," it was years afterward "before I understood what being in love was or what loving really meant."

But if she was more certain of his feeling for her than of hers for him, she had (as her memoirs testify) no

*Eleanor in her bridal gown, March, 1905*

serene confidence that his desire for her was strong enough, tenacious enough to survive the covert, subtle, yet determined onslaught of her prospective mother-in-law. Hence, in proportion to her wish for marriage, a wish which may in large part have been a yearning for the unprecedented security she felt she would have in the bosom of the Delano clan, she suffered anxiety during the weeks of Franklin's Caribbean cruise. He seemed so malleable in his mother's hands!

Fortunately, she was enabled to spend the weeks of waiting, not amidst the (to her) boring banalities of New York society, but in the very different, the much more interesting and less trivial society of Washington, D. C. She was in New York on February 16, 1904, when Pussie was married to W. Forbes Morgan, Jr.— an occasion that made few of the bride's family and close friends "very happy," as Eleanor later wrote, because the groom "was a number of years younger than Pussie," and none who knew the latter well be-

lieved her capable of adjusting "to the complicated business of married life." But Eleanor's Auntie Bye asked her down to Washington for the winter months of 1904; and Auntie Bye —sister of the President, wife of an admiral—was not only very much in the mainstream of the capital's social affairs but was also a confidante and, on some matters of state, a respected adviser of Uncle Ted. He, the President, came now and then to his sister's house, where he talked freely, volubly. Eleanor was an overnight guest once or twice at the White House. Thus she gained some inkling of the private life and self of a public man who had come to occupy an office of supreme power. She gained other knowledge as well. She accompanied her aunt on the latter's round of afternoon calls ("I was aghast at this obligation") and was a guest at almost daily luncheons, teas, and dinners where she met diplomats, high government officials, politicians, visiting celebrities—people who were actually doing important things in the great world and who had "charm and wit and *savoir faire.*" She found herself unwontedly at ease in this company. She realized further what she had begun to realize during her European schooling, namely, that she had a mind that was quick, capacious, and retentive, and that she was an interesting conversationalist, able to use the smattering of information she had gained in various fields in such a way as to give her listener, frequently an authority in one of those fields, the impression that she was far more knowledgeable than actually she was.

She blossomed in this environment. She gained swiftly in self-confidence and poise, so that she no doubt would have been able to bear, not breaking under it, the disappointment of her hopes for marriage to Franklin Roosevelt, had this been required of her.

It was not required. Franklin left the cruise at Nassau and came up to the capital from Florida by train.

Thereafter he spent most of his several days in Washington with Eleanor; he was as ardent and determined a lover as ever.

The engagement of Franklin Delano Roosevelt to marry Anna Eleanor Roosevelt was formally announced in late November, 1904.

By that time Franklin had been enrolled for more than two months as a student in the Columbia University Law School and was living with his mother in a house she had rented at 200 Madison Avenue in New York City. Some three weeks before, he had journeyed to Hyde Park to cast his first ballot in a Presidential election. Despite his father's and his own lifelong Democracy, he had "voted for the Republican candidate, Theodore Roosevelt, because I thought he was a better Democrat than the Democratic candidate," as he said thirty-odd years later.

By that time, too, Franklin had informed Endicott Peabody by letter that his engagement to "my distant cousin . . . is about to come out" and had expressed the "hope," Eleanor's as well as his own, "that you will be able to help us in the ceremony—it wouldn't be the same without you." Of his own immediate occupation he wrote with something less than enthusiasm. He said he was in law school "trying to understand a little of the work," adding that "of course I am going to keep right on"—as if in spite of doubts, boredom, and a sense of personal inadequacy.

And he did "keep right on," though with a bare minimum of that prolonged, concentrated study required of law students. Indeed, he evidently did less than the required minimum in two of his courses, one of them the highly important "Contracts," which he failed at the end of his first year, to his great surprise, for he had believed himself to be doing as well in the failed subjects as in the others, in each of which he received the very respectable grade of B. It became necessary for him to take make-up examinations in the two subjects the following fall if he was to stay with his class.

His vital interests, during that first law-school year, centered in the house on East Seventy-sixth Street—the Parish house—where Eleanor lived. He spent as much time with her as he possibly could, going often with her to social events. On March 4, 1905, he and she were present by special invitation at the inauguration of Theodore Roosevelt as President. They were very much at the center of the ceremonies and festivities of this historic event. They had come down to Washington in the private railway car of a cousin, George Emlen Roosevelt; they sat on the Capitol steps behind the Theodore Roosevelt family as the President took the oath of office and delivered his inaugural address; they lunched afterward at the White House before going out to the official reviewing stand to watch the inaugural parade; and of course they danced together at the inaugural ball that night.

Thirteen days later, on Saint Patrick's Day, which was also the birthday of Eleanor's mother, they were married.

The wedding took place, as Pussie's had, in the home of Mrs. E. Livingston Ludlow, who was Pussie's aunt and Mrs. Henry Parish's mother. The Ludlow house adjoined the Parishes' on East Seventy-sixth Street, between Madison and Fifth avenues, and the drawing rooms of the two were separated only by sliding doors that could be opened for special occasions to make the two large rooms into one enormous one. This had been done for Pussie's wedding; it was to be done for Eleanor's wedding reception after the ceremony itself, at which attendance was restricted to the two families and a few of the most intimate friends.

The bride wore a long-sleeved dress of stiff white satin, with shirred tulle at the neck—a dress covered by her Grandmother Hall's rose-point Brussels lace, of which the long bridal veil was also made. Around her throat was a dog collar of pearls given her by Franklin's mother; in her arms was a huge bouquet of lilies of the valley. She was radiant, almost beautiful, and certainly graceful in her tall slenderness as she emerged from the upstairs bedroom where she had dressed, came down the stairway on the arm of her escort, and walked slowly along the aisle between the groom's assembled family and her own to the chancel of pink roses and palms that had been set up before the fireplace. The groom awaited her there, with his best man, Lathrop Brown, as did the Reverend Dr. Peabody, who performed the ceremony.

But the center of attention at this wedding and reception was not the bride. Not for her sake, nor that of the man she was to marry, did great crowds gather at both the Fifth and Madison Avenue entrances to that block, entrances cordoned off by more than seventy-five policemen who permitted none but invited guests to enter and, indeed, so zealously checked their credentials that several did not get into the Ludlow-Parish houses until after the reception had almost ended. When the bride came down the stairs she was less stared at even by that family assemblage than was the man who was the object of all this police guardianship—a bespectacled, mustached man almost a head shorter than she, upon whose arm she leaned—and the most memorable moment of the ceremony came, not when the Reverend Dr. Peabody pronounced Franklin and Eleanor man and wife, but when he asked, "Who giveth this woman to be married to this man?" and was answered by the stocky bespectacled man, in a loud voice, "I do!" For this man who gave the bride away—

this man for whose convenience the wedding date had been set (in his official capacity he had reviewed the Saint Patrick's Day Parade up Fifth Avenue before coming to the Parish-Ludlow houses)—was none other than Eleanor's Uncle Ted, the President of the United States.

The sliding doors were opened. The throng on the Parish side of them, awaiting the reception, pressed through toward the chancel where the bridal couple stood. There the President of the United States was heard to congratulate his niece and distant cousin, saying he was delighted that they were keeping the Roosevelt name in the family. Then he strode into the Parish library where refreshments were being served and where he, no doubt (for he was one of the great trenchermen of that overstuffed age), partook heartily of them. The guests followed him. Soon the young married couple were left all alone before the altar, gazing perhaps a bit ruefully at each other, though Eleanor would later remember that neither she nor Franklin was particularly surprised or dismayed by this desertion. They simply followed the others into the library where Uncle Ted held forth with jokes and stories, and where they listened and laughed with the rest.

After the President's departure and the reception's end, Franklin and Eleanor slipped away, donned travelling clothes, and entrained for Hyde Park, where they had a short week of honeymooning before moving into an apartment they had rented in the Hotel Webster, on West Forty-fifth Street. Here they lived until Franklin completed his first year of law school.

*This article is based on a biography of Franklin D. Roosevelt to be published by G. P. Putnam's Sons in 1972 or 1973. Mr. Davis is the author of* The Politics of Honor *(1967), a biography of Adlai Stevenson; and of* Experience of War *(1965), a study of World War* II.

# DISASTER
# AT BARI

*It was the most devastating enemy surprise
attack since Pearl Harbor — but what mysterious
affliction were people dying of two days later?*

*By* GLENN INFIELD

The port of Bari, Italy, was crowded on the afternoon of December 2, 1943, when Captain Otto Heitmann returned to his ship, the *John Bascom*, with the two thousand dollars he had drawn from the U.S. Army Finance Section to pay his crew. Bari was a pleasant, peaceful city on the heel of the peninsula, little changed by the war except that in 1943 American and British military personnel crowded Victor Emmanuel Street and Corso Cavour instead of the Germans, who had been forced to flee northward. Usually Heitmann enjoyed the time he had to spend at this port on the Adriatic Sea while his Liberty Ship was unloaded, but he was nervous this December day. There were too many ships in the harbor. Without even lifting his binoculars to his eyes he could see the *Joseph Wheeler, Hadley F. Brown, Pumper, Aroostook, John L. Motley, Samuel J. Tilden,* and *Devon Coast,* all jammed in the main section of the harbor or along the east jetty. He had been told there were at least twenty-nine ships at Bari waiting for aviation fuel, bombs, ammunition, hospital equipment, and other military supplies to be unloaded. The *John Harvey,* a Liberty Ship captained by his acquaintance Elwin P. Knowles, was anchored at pier 29. Heitmann idly wondered what she was carrying, unaware that the secret cargo aboard the *John Harvey* had already set the stage for tragedy at Bari.

"Look!"

Heitmann stared skyward in the direction his second officer, William Rudolph, was pointing. There, high in the sky where the last rays of

*Hours after the attack on Bari, Allied ships were still burning and sinking. Despite the total surprise achieved by the German bombers, two out of the 105 planes that took part were shot down by hastily manned antiaircraft guns like those in the foreground.*

*Bari's well-defined harbor made a neat target for the incoming German planes. At the time of the raid it was far more crowded with shipping than when this peaceful scene was photographed.*

the sun glinted on its wings, was a lone plane crossing directly over the crowded harbor.

High above Bari harbor in the plane, Oberleutnant Werner Hahn counted the Allied ships in port and knew the time had come. The Luftwaffe reconnaissance pilot banked his plane northward and hurried back toward his home base to report.

While Heitmann was standing on the deck of his ship in the harbor watching the plane high above him, General James H. "Jimmy" Doolittle was busy in his Fifteenth Air Force headquarters building along the waterfront. The man who had become famous as leader of the raid on Tokyo in 1942 was struggling with the multitude of problems involved with a new organization. All day long he had heard C-47's flying in men and supplies for

his air force, and the sound of one more aircraft didn't interest him. What did interest him was getting the B-17's and B-24's at the Foggia airfield complex, seventy miles to the north, into operation as soon as feasible. The possibility of a German air raid on Bari was out of the question. Hadn't British Air Marshal Sir Arthur Coningham, commanding officer of the British air forces in the area, assured everyone that very afternoon that the Luftwaffe did not have the resources to attack the city or the harbor? "I would regard it as a personal affront and insult if the Luftwaffe should attempt any significant action in this area," Coningham had stated. So even when the lights were turned on along the harbor for the unloading that would continue through the night—positive proof that the British, who controlled the harbor, "knew" it was secure from enemy attack—Doolittle wasn't apprehensive.

As the lights were turned on at Bari harbor, 105 Ju-88 bombers led by Oberleutnant Gustav Teuber swung west far out over the Adriatic Sea and headed straight for Bari. Teuber's estimated time of arrival over the harbor was 7:30 P.M.

In the city many of the inhabitants were hurrying toward the Chiesa San Domenico opera house on Victor Emmanuel Street. The evening concerts were a part of Italian culture and were held regardless of which nation controlled the country. The fishermen and their families who lived in the old section of the city near the waterfront, however, seldom could afford the concerts. The younger members usually went to Bambino Stadium to watch the Americans play baseball or football. The older inhabitants often went to Mass in the Basilica of San Nicola, the church built to honor St. Nicholas, better known in many parts of the world as Santa Claus. The sick and disabled stayed at home among the narrow, winding streets bordered by one- and two-storied houses jammed close together. Old Bari had few escape routes from it . . . and those who lived there would soon need them all.

Fifty miles east of Bari, Oberleutnant Teuber looked at his watch. It was 7:15 P.M. He could not yet see the glow of the harbor through the cockpit window of his Ju-88, but he knew they were getting close to their target —the Allied ships in Bari harbor. He gently nosed his plane down to wave-top level, and the other aircraft followed. They were now below the radar defenses of the city.

As the German bombers roared in, ten minutes later, Teuber saw the ships lined up in Bari harbor and gasped. It was unbelievable. He did not have time to count them, but there were targets everywhere he looked. Selecting one of the ships, he called to his bombardier: "Prepare to drop bombs!" The ship he had selected was the *John Harvey.*

The first bomb explosions were off target and hit in the city, but as Captain Heitmann watched aboard the *John Bascom,* Teuber and his fellow pilots discovered their error and began "walking" the bombs out into the water toward the ships. Yard by yard the bombs came closer, working their way up the line of moored ships one by one. The *Joseph Wheeler* took a direct hit and burst into flames; moments later the *John L. Motley,* anchored next to Heitmann's ship, took a bomb on its number-five hatch, and the deck cargo caught fire. It was too late to move the *John Bascom.* Suddenly a string of explosions ripped the ship from fore to aft, and Heitmann was lifted completely off his feet and slammed hard against the wheel-house door. The door broke off its hinges, and both the captain and the door hit the deck.

At pier 29 a small fire had started on board the *John Harvey.*

General Doolittle was leafing through a report on his desk when his office suddenly became much brighter. Before he could get to his feet, the windows on the side of the office facing the harbor shattered, and the glass flew across the room, narrowly missing him. Hurrying to the opening where the glass had been a minute before, Doolittle looked out at the harbor. One look was enough. His men, his supplies, his equipment for the Fifteenth Air Force were gone.

The citizens of Bari, unaccustomed to air attacks, were confused and frightened. Those who were in the opera house were unharmed, but many were panic-stricken. In the old city, people hurried from the Basilica of San Nicola where they had been attending Mass when the first explosions sounded. They had just reached the street when another stick of bombs hit nearby. Hundreds were now racing through the old section of Bari, trying to escape the narrow streets where flames made it nearly impossible to breathe. Their immediate concern was to get away, even if it meant drawing closer to the burning ships in the harbor. They dashed wildly, running into each other, knocking children to the street in their headlong rush to what they thought was safety. Many of them reached the edge of the harbor moments before the flames on the *John Harvey* reached the cargo the ship was carrying.

The explosion of the *John Harvey* shook the entire harbor. Clouds of smoke, tinted every color of the rainbow, shot thousands of feet into the air. Meteoric sheets of metal rocketed in all directions, carrying incendiary torches to other ships and setting off a series of explosions that made the harbor a holocaust. Jimmy Doolittle, still standing by the shattered window of his office, was staggered by the terrific blast. Huddled on the east jetty, Heitmann and other survivors from the ships in the harbor were bathed in the bright light momentarily and then bombarded by debris, oil, and dirty water. The inhabitants of old Bari who had rushed to the harbor to escape the flames within the walls of the ancient section were gathered along the shore when the *John Harvey* exploded. There was no time to run, no time to hide, no time for anything. One moment they were rejoicing in their good fortune in escaping from the flames of the old city; the next they were struck by the unbearable concussion of the blast. Some were blown upward, their broken bodies flying twenty-five to thirty feet high. Some were hurtled straight back the way they had come.

A short time after the *John Harvey* exploded, Deck Cadet James L. Cahill, a member of the ship's crew who had been on shore leave, reached dockside. He looked around wildly.

"She's gone!" he exclaimed. "The *John Harvey* is gone!"

A British major standing nearby looked at the distressed crewman. "A pity. What did she carry?"

"Ammunition, I think." Cahill's face clouded. "And . . . and . . ."

"Yes?"

"I don't know. Nobody knew. It was a big secret."

The "secret" to which the deck cadet referred became vital within twenty-four hours at the various hospitals in the Bari area where the hundreds of victims were taken. At the Three New Zealand General Hospital, the Ninety-eight British General Hospital, and the American Twenty-six General Hospital, the horde of incoming patients filled all available beds, and many were placed in vacant rooms that were still not equipped for use. The nurses and doctors were overwhelmed but did their best to treat the victims for their injuries and the obvious shock most of them had suffered. At least they could be wrapped in blankets. Unfortunately, many of the survivors were still in their dirty wet clothes the next day when a striking variation from the normal symptons of shock was noticed by the medical personnel. Nearly all the patients had eye troubles. Weeping became very marked and was associated with spasms of the eyelids and a morbid fear of light. Many of the survivors complained that they were blind.

Other puzzling factors were the pulse and blood pressure readings of the patients supposedly in shock or suffering from immersion and exposure. The pulse beat was barely evident, and blood pressure was extremely low; yet the patients did not appear to be in what doctors call clinical shock. There was no worried or anxious expression or restlessness, no shallow breathing, and the heart action was only a moderately rapid 110–120.

On the morning following the German air raid, skin lesions were noticed on many of the survivors. The coloration of the lesion area was most striking: bronze, reddish brown, or tan on some victims, red on others. The distribution of the burns was varied, but a certain pattern began to emerge. It seemed to depend upon the degree of exposure to the slimy waters of the harbor. Those who had been completely immersed were burned all over, but those who had gotten only their feet or arms in the water were burned nowhere else. Survivors who had been splashed by the water had lesions where the water hit them. And those who had washed the slime from the harbor waters off their bodies and put on clean clothes had no burns at all.

The doctors and nurses did everything they could think of for the victims, but none of the normal treatments for burns or shock or exposure aided the survivors. They would improve temporarily, take a sudden turn for the worse, and then abruptly die for no apparent reason. By the end of the second day after the Bari at-

tack it was clear that outside help was needed: the mysterious deaths among both military and civilian casualties were increasing.

Allied Force Headquarters in Algiers, under the command of General Dwight D. Eisenhower, was aware of the disastrous air strike made by the Luftwaffe at Bari. However, it wasn't until General Fred Blesse, deputy surgeon for Allied Force Headquarters, received a "red light" call from Italy that anyone outside the Bari area was alerted to the mysterious malady that was causing so many deaths. He immediately dispatched Lieutenant Colonel Stewart F. Alexander to Italy to investigate.

Alexander, a graduate of Columbia University College of Physicians and Surgeons, had served as medical officer with General George S. Patton, Jr., had been one of the few medical officers present at the Casablanca conference, had later joined the staff of General Mark W. Clark, and had finally moved to Algiers and the Allied Force Headquarters after having been selected by Eisenhower for his staff. Alexander had also worked at the Medical Research Division of the Edgewood Arsenal, Maryland, before going overseas. The knowledge gained there would be invaluable at Bari.

On reaching Bari, Alexander immediately toured the area military hospitals, consulting with the medical staffs and examining the casualties. As he stepped into the first hospital, he turned to the British officer accompanying him and asked one question: "What is that odor? Garlic?"

"No, it's from the patients. We haven't had time to disinfect the wards since their arrival from the harbor."

Alexander remembered the long hours of research at Edgewood Arsenal: the same odor had permeated his laboratory there. Yet he couldn't believe that the odor in the hospital came from the same source. Surely not.

As he examined the small blisters on the patients, however, Alexander saw more evidence that fitted in with the strange odor. The fluid accumulations of the blisters in the superficial layers of the skin were diffused, and in many cases it was difficult to determine where the edges of the blisters were located. He checked x rays taken of the victims and discovered that very few of the patients with the mysterious symptoms had suffered blast damage to their lungs, yet they had lower-respiratory-tract symptoms. He watched one patient, who appeared to be in marked shock but was remarkably clear mentally, tell a nurse he was feeling much better—and then die seconds later without any indication of distress at the time of death. Alexander was now convinced that his initial theory was correct.

"I feel that these men may have been exposed to mus-

CONTINUED ON PAGE 104

# URBAN POLLUTION-Many long years ago

*The old gray mare was not the ecological marvel,*
*in American cities, that horse lovers like to believe*

*Though the car was on its way—note the auto-show billboard—the horse was still the prime mover and litterer in New York about 1910.*
BROWN BROTHERS

To many urban Americans in the 1970's, fighting their way through the traffic's din and gagging on air heavy with exhaust fumes, the automobile is a major villain in the sad tale of atmospheric pollution. Yet they have forgotten, or rather never knew, that the predecessor of the auto was also a major polluter. The faithful, friendly horse was charged with creating the very problems today attributed to the automobile: air contaminants harmful to health, noxious odors, and noise. At the be-

ginning of the twentieth century, in fact, writers in popular and scientific periodicals were decrying the pollution of the public streets and demanding "the banishment of the horse from American cities" in vigorous terms. The presence of 120,000 horses in New York City, wrote one 1908 authority for example, is "an economic burden, an affront to cleanliness, and a terrible tax upon human life." The solution to the problem, agreed the critics, was the adoption of the "horseless carriage."

A concern with clean streets and with the horse as a principal obstacle to them was nothing new. European cities had shown concern for the problem as early as the fourteenth century, as had American cities from their beginnings. But it required a more statistically minded age to measure the actual amount of manure produced by the horse. Sanitary experts in the early part of the twentieth century agreed that the normal city horse produced between fifteen and thirty pounds of manure a day,

*By* JOEL A. TARR

with the average being something like twenty-two pounds. In a city like Milwaukee in 1907, for instance, with a human population of 350,000 and a horse population of 12,500, this meant 133 tons of manure a day, for a daily average of nearly three-quarters of a pound of manure for each resident. Or, as health officials in Rochester, New York, calculated in 1900, the fifteen thousand horses in that city produced enough manure in a year to make a pile 175 feet high covering an acre of ground and breeding sixteen billion flies, each one a potential spreader of germs.

Milwaukee and Rochester resembled other American cities in 1900 in having thousands of horses at work in their streets even after the automobile and electric streetcar had been introduced. Chicago had 83,-330, Detroit 12,000, and Columbus 5,000. Overall, there were probably between three and three and a half million horses in American cities as the century opened, compared with about seventeen million living in more bucolic environments. (Today, at a time when horseback riding for pleasure is on the rise, the total number of horses in the United States is somewhat over seven million.) The ratio of horses to people was much higher in cities where traction lines were not yet completely electrified. In 1890, even after electrification

*Pedestrian perils in the age of the horse included the plunging hooves of skittish animals. This is Broadway, New York, in 1853.*

had already begun, twenty-two thousand horses and mules were still required simply for pulling streetcars in New York City and in Brooklyn, with a total of ten thousand performing similarly in Philadelphia and Chicago. Ten years earlier, when New York and Brooklyn had counted no electric railways and 1,764,168 souls, they had a total equine population of 150,000 to 175,000.

To a great extent nineteenth-century urban life moved at the pace of horse-drawn transportation, and the evidence of the horse was everywhere —in the piles of manure that littered the streets attracting swarms of flies and creating stench, in the iron rings and hitching posts sunk into the pavements for fastening horses' reins, and in the numerous livery stables that gave off a mingled smell of horse urine and manure, harness oil and hay. In 1880 New York and Brooklyn were served by 427 blacksmith shops, 249 carriage and wagon enterprises, 262 wheelwright shops, and 290 establishments dealing in saddles and harnesses. They were eminently necessary. On a typical day in 1885 an engineer, Francis V. Greene, making a study of urban traffic conditions, counted 7,811 horse-drawn vehicles, many with teams of two or more horses, passing the busy corner of Broadway and Pine Street.

While some of these conveyances were fine carriages drawn by spirited teams, the most common city horses were commercial or work animals. City streets were crowded with large team-pulled drays guided by husky and colorfully profane drivers and piled high with heavy freight. Among these, single-horse spring wagons twisted their way, making deliveries of ice, milk, and goods of every kind to residential areas. Their sides were often brightly decorated with advertisements, catching the eyes of passers-by and of the riders in the many omnibuses and hacks plying their routes. The horse remained essential in urban civilization, even after the

development of the steam engine. As the *Nation* noted in 1872, though great improvements had been made in the development of such "agents of progress" as the railroad, the steamboat, and the telegraph, modern society's dependence on the horse had "grown almost *pari passu* with our dependence on steam." For it was the horse who fed the railroads and steamboats with passengers and freight, and who provided transportation within the cities.

Yet this hard-working animal, so vital to the functioning of urban society, posed problems that were recognized by even the earliest American city dwellers. The question of clean streets was most obvious. In eighteenth-century Boston and New York, money was allocated by the city fathers for street cleaning, and householders were required to sweep the road in front of their doorways. Cities made sporadic attempts during the mid-nineteenth century to mechanize the tasks of sanitation. In 1855 New York introduced street-sweeping machines and self-loading carts, and in 1865 urban entrepreneurs formed the New York Sanitary and Chemical Compost Manufacturing Company for the purpose of "cleansing cities, towns, and villages in the United States" with several varieties of mechanical devices adapted to the task. By 1880 almost all cities over thirty thousand in population employed street-cleaners.

American cities made their most sustained efforts to clean the streets under the stimulus of the fear induced by epidemics of cholera, smallpox, yellow fever, or typhoid. Many eighteenth- and nineteenth-century medical authorities believed that such diseases were caused by "a combination of certain atmospheric conditions and putrefying filth," among which horse manure was a chief offender. In 1752 Boston selectmen allocated extra funds to clean the streets because of the fear that street dirt might contain smallpox infection, and in 1795, during the yellow-fever season, town officials invited neighboring farmers to collect the manure from the streets free of charge. The city fathers of New York, faced by the threat of cholera in 1832, made special efforts to cleanse the cobblestones, thereby divesting the city "of that foul aliment on which the pestilence delights to feed."

But unless jolted by rampant disease, city authorities and citizens tolerated a great deal of "that foul aliment" in their streets. One reason, perhaps, was a reluctance to spend money on such an unsatisfying, if crucial, municipal effort. Some cities tried to cover the cost of street cleaning by selling the manure for fertilizer. In 1803 the New York superintendent of scavengers expended about twenty-six thousand dollars for street cleaning and realized over twenty-nine thousand dollars from the sale of the manure collected. Despite this instance of profitable purifying, however, paid scavenging did not generally achieve great results. In those cases where private contractors were responsible for cleaning the streets, citizens often complained that they neglected other forms of rubbish and only collected the salable manure. Nor did a shift to public sanitation service improve things. Officials of post-Civil War years often reported that street dirt was becoming too mixed with other forms of litter to be sold as fertilizer. Moreover, whatever the salable quality of the street refuse, urban sanitation departments during the nineteenth century were notoriously inefficient. Vexed by graft and corruption, they were staffed by "old and indigent men," "prisoners who don't like to work," and "persons on relief."

Street cleaning, therefore, remained largely inadequate, and one is thus not surprised to discover that newspapers, diaries, and governmental reports abound with complaints about the problems created in the city by

*Although some of the elements in this 1881 political cartoon were a bit esoteric, nobody needed an explanation of the principal symbol, the big pile of horse manure.*
CULVER PICTURES

horse manure left in the public thoroughfares. Manure collected into unattended piles by the street cleaners bred huge numbers of flies and created "pestilential vapours." Offal was sometimes carried from wealthy residential neighborhoods and dumped in poor neighborhoods, where it was left to rot. Streets turned into virtual cesspools when it rained, and long-skirted ladies suffered the indignity of trailing their hems in liquefied manure. In London, ladies and gentlemen were aided in their navigation through a sea of horse droppings by "crossing-sweepers," but no such group appeared in more democratic American cities. Yet dry weather was no great improvement, for then there were complaints of the "pulverized horse dung" that blew into people's faces and the windows of their homes, and over the outdoor displays of merchants' wares. The coming of paved streets accelerated this problem, as wheels and hoofs ground the sun-dried manure against the hard surfaces and amplified the amount of dust.

And then there was noise. In many American cities, early paving consisted largely of cobblestones, on which the clopping and clanking of horses' iron shoes and the iron-tired

wheels of carts and wagons created an immense din. Benjamin Franklin complained in the late eighteenth century of the "thundering of coaches, chariots, chaises, waggons, drays and the whole fraternity of noise" that assailed the ears of Philadelphians. Similar comments about urban noise were made by travellers in other cities. Attempts were made quite early to quiet the clamor. In 1747, in Boston, the town council banned traffic from King Street so that the noise would not distract the deliberations of the General Court. In 1785 New York City passed an ordinance forbidding teams and wagons with iron-shod wheels from the streets. In London good medical management required the putting of straw on the pavement outside sick people's houses to muffle the sounds of traffic, a practice undoubtedly followed in America. Yet the problem grew with the growing nation. As late as the 1890's a writer in *Scientific American* noted that the sounds of traffic on busy New York streets made conversation nearly impossible, while the author William Dean Howells complained that "the sharp clatter of the horses' iron shoes" on the pavement tormented his ear.

If the horse, by his biological necessities, created problems for the city, the city, in turn, was a harsh environment for the animals whose possession had once been the mark and privilege of nobility. The horse belonged to the open spaces and the battlefield. In an urban setting he was, with rare exception, a drudge. City horses were notoriously overworked. The average streetcar nag had a life expectancy of barely two years, and it was a common sight to see drivers and teamsters savagely lashing their overburdened animals. The mistreatment of city horses was a key factor in moving Henry Bergh to found the American Society for the Prevention of Cruelty to Animals in 1866. When released from harness, the working steed usually was led to a crowded and unsanitary stable without adequate light or air. Only the pleasure horses kept by the city's "swells" to drive handsome rigs in the park had access to the green fields enjoyed by their country cousins.

Many overworked, mistreated urban horses simply died in the city streets. Moreover, since asphalt-paved or cobbled streets were slipperier than dirt roads, horses often stumbled and fell. An unfortunate beast who broke a leg in this way was destroyed where it lay. (In order to minimize the risk of stumbles, some veterinarians recommended that city draft horses be shod with rubber-padded horseshoes, but few owners followed this advice.) A description of Broadway appearing in the *Atlantic Monthly* in 1866 spoke of the street as being clogged with "dead horses and vehicular entanglements." The equine carcasses added fearsomely to the smells and flies already rising in clouds from stables and manure piles. In 1880 New York City removed fifteen thousand dead horses from its streets, and as late as 1912 Chicago carted away nearly ten thousand horse carcasses. A contemporary book on the collection of municipal refuse advised that, since the average weight of a dead horse was thirteen hundred pounds, "trucks for the removal of dead horses should be hung low, to avoid an excessive lift." The complaint of one horse

lover that "in the city the working horse is treated worse than a steam-engine or sewing machine," was well justified.

By the 1880's and 90's the immense population growth of American cities, the need for improved urban transportation to keep up with the geographic spread of communities, and a growing awareness of the need for better sanitation in the interest of public health, all emphasized the drawbacks of the horse as the chief form of urban locomotion and spurred a search for alternatives. The first major breakthrough came with the development of the cable car and the electric trolley car in the late 1880's. Traction companies were quick to substitute mechanical power for animal power on their streetcar lines. Writing in *Popular Science Monthly* in 1892, United States Commissioner of Labor Carroll D. Wright maintained that electric power was not only cheaper than horsepower, but also far more beneficial to the city from the perspective of health and safety. "The presence of so many horses constantly moving through the streets," wrote Wright somewhat ponderously, "is a very serious matter. The vitiation of the air by the presence of so many animals is alone a sufficient reason for their removal, while the clogged condition of the streets impedes business, and involves the safety of life and limb." While electric-powered transportation began to make inroads on the horse's

domain, improvements in the gasoline engine made it clear that the automobile would soon be a viable alternative. Even the bicycle craze of the nineties reminded many that horseless commuting was possible over reasonable distances.

Horse lovers became defensive about the future of that quadruped. Writing in the *Chautauquan* in 1895, Robert L. Seymour maintained that while the "cheap horse" might be doomed, the "costly, good-looking horse, the horse of history, the heroic horse in action, will probably last long." Can you imagine, asked Seymour, "Napoleon crossing the Alps in a blinding snow storm on a bicycle or Alexander riding heroically at the head of his armies in a horseless carriage?" It is hard to blame Seymour for not having the prophetic gift to foresee tank commanders dashing ahead of their squadrons. A more fundamental error seems to have been made by a writer in *Lippincott's Magazine* who insisted that since "Americans are a horse-loving nation . . . the wide-spread adoption of the motor-driven vehicle in this country is open to serious doubt." Less romantic observers, however, embraced the possibility of the elimination of the horse with enthusiasm. When William Dean Howells' fictional traveller from the nonexistent, utopian land of Altruria visited Chicago's World's Fair of 1893, he noted with pleasure that this metropolis of the future had "little of the filth re-

sulting in all other American cities from the use of the horse."

During the opening years of the twentieth century the movement toward salvation by internal combustion continued to gather headway. Such popular journals as *Harper's Weekly*, *Lippincott's Magazine*, and the *Forum*, as well as more specialized periodicals like *American City*, *Horseless Age*, *Motor*, and *Scientific American*, were filled with articles extolling the automobile and the motor truck and disparaging the horse. There were several lines of attack. One of the most common was economic analysis, which argued, as did one writer in *Munsey's Magazine*, that "the horse has become unprofitable. He is too costly to buy and too costly to keep." Articles such as these computed the expense of the "horse cost of living" and compared it unfavorably to the expense of automobile upkeep. Other articles pointed out the advantages the motor truck had over the horse in hauling freight and in preventing traffic tie-ups by moving faster. One writer in *American City* noted that the good motor truck, which was immune to fatigue and to weather, did on the average of two and a half times as much work in the same time as the horse and with one-quarter the amount of street congestion. "It is all a question of dollars and cents, this gasoline or oats proposition. The automobile is no longer classed as a luxury. It is acknowledged to be one of the great time-savers in the world."

But a second and equally—if not more—convincing argument for the superiority of the motor vehicle over the horse rested on the testimony that the automobile was a better bet from the perspective of public medicine. "The horse in the city is bound to be a menace to a condition of perfect health," warned Dr. Arthur R. Reynolds, superintendent of the Chicago health department in 1901. Public health officials in various cities charged that wind-blown dust from ground-up manure damaged eyes and irritated respiratory organs, while the "noise and clatter" of city traffic aggravated nervous diseases. Since, noted *Scientific American*, the motor vehicle left no litter and was "always noiseless or nearly so" (a judgment hard to understand if one has heard a primitive auto engine), the exit of the horse would "benefit the public health to an almost incalculable degree."

Also blamed on the horse were such familiar plagues as cholera and typhoid fever and intestinal diseases like dysentery and infant diarrhea. The reason why faithful dobbin was adjudged guilty was that such diseases were often transmitted by the housefly, and the favorite breeding place of the fly was the manure heap. In the late 1890's insurance company actuaries discovered that employees in livery stables and those living near stables had a higher rate of infectious diseases, such as typhoid fever, than the general public. Sanitation specialists pursued the question, and the first decade of the twentieth century saw a large outpouring of material warning of the danger of the infection-carrying "queen of the dung-heap," *Musca domestica*. The most obvious way to eradicate the "typhoid fly," as the carrier was called by L. O. Howard, chief of the Bureau of Entomology of the Department of Agriculture and a leader of a campaign to stamp out flies, was to eliminate the horse.

Writing in *Appleton's Magazine* in 1908, Harold Bolce entitled his article "The Horse Vs. Health." In a thoroughgoing assault he blamed most of the sanitary and economic problems of the modern city on the horse and essayed to calculate the savings if all horses were replaced by automobiles and motor trucks. His figures were arrived at by an intriguing formula. According to Bolce, twenty thousand New Yorkers died each year from "maladies that fly in the dust" created mainly by horse manure. He estimated the monetary value to the community of these people's lives, plus the cost of maintaining hospitals to treat them, and laid the entire bill on the withers of the inoffensive horse. To this sum he added the cost of street cleaning and rubbish disposal. He also attributed a higher urban cost of living to the failure to use speedy motor trucks, instead of horses, in transporting goods. Finally he computed and added the costs of traffic congestion and reached a total of approximately one hundred million dollars as the price that New York City paid for not banning the horse from its streets. What fed Bolce's indignation was not so much hate of horses, perhaps, as dedication to progress. The horse, he maintained, represented one of the last stands of brute animal strength over applied science and, as such, had to go—Americans could no longer afford "the absurdities of a horse-infected city."

While no city ever took such drastic action as banning horses completely from its boundaries, many cities did eventually forbid them the use of certain streets and highways. But in the long run the horse's opponents triumphed without recourse to legislation. The number of horses in cities dropped sharply as the automobile and the motor truck rapidly gained popularity, although the number of horses in the nation stayed high until the 1920's (there were 20,091,000 horses reported in the 1920 census). As this happened, the benefits promised by motor-vehicle enthusiasts seemed to be initially realized. Streets were cleaner, particle pollution resulting from ground-up manure and the diseases thereby produced were diminished, the number of flies was greatly reduced, goods were transported more cheaply and efficiently, traffic travelled at a faster rate, and the movement of people from crowded cities to sub-

CONTINUED ON PAGE 106

Charles Marion Russell, the famous artist of the American West, came to Montana in 1880 as a boy of sixteen. He lived there the rest of his life, working for a number of years as a cattle wrangler and gradually getting to know with intimacy the men and the country that were to be his great subject during forty-six years of drawing, painting, and sculpting.

It is always interesting to see the early efforts of an artist who later became a master. Below and on the following pages are a few samples, some never before published, of sketches made by Charlie Russell when he was only fifteen. It was later on in that same year, 1880, that he travelled to Montana for the first time. It was decisive: he put school and the Middle West and East behind him forever.

The boyish sketchbook represented here was lost track of for a long time. It now belongs to Mr. R. D. Warden, of Great Falls, Montana, with whose cooperation we made the accompanying selections, and who also arranged for the publication of the article beginning on this page by Mr. Frederic G. Renner of Washington, D.C., a foremost expert on Russell. Mr. Renner's article describes how the sketches were authenticated. —The Editors

# A SCHOOLBOY'S SKETCHBOOK

## By FREDERIC G. RENNER

I am not absolutely certain of the year, but I believe it was in 1953 that Mr. Otto Veerhoff, proprietor of the Veerhoff Galleries in Washington, D.C., asked me to drop by to see something that he thought would be of considerable interest to me. My first thought was that he might have a Russell drawing or water color for sale, as I knew he was aware of my deep interest in the works of this artist. However, he wouldn't tell me what it was over the telephone and added to the small mystery with the remark that I would have to see and judge for myself. From this I assumed that what had turned up was probably a painting of a western scene of some kind, possibly unsigned, and that Mr. Veerhoff merely wanted my opinion as to whether or not it might have been done by Russell.

A day or two later I visited the Veerhoff Galleries and had a small portfolio of sketches placed in my hands. The book was old, the covers scuffed, and some of the pages loose. It looked as if it might have originally been intended for an old-fashioned penmanship copybook. Inside were twenty-six full-page pencil drawings of various frontier scenes and characters, all but five of them signed C M R. There were drawings of Indians of several tribes, cowboys, hunters, prospectors, gamblers, and Mexicans. These were certainly the kinds of subjects that Russell might have drawn, and the titles under each one of them gave every appearance of being in Russell's hand.

However, even a casual examination raised a number of questions. The sketches were exceedingly crude, poorer and more primitive than any of Russell's drawings that I had ever seen. There were also obvious mistakes in some of them. An Indian pony in one sketch appeared to be wearing a bridle. In another the thong used to guide the animal was around the horse's nose instead of the lower jaw, and on the left side of the horse's neck. Whoever had made the drawing had obviously been unaware that Indians usually mounted from the right side, rather than white-man style, from the left. Still another drawing showed three mounted Indian men moving camp with travois, work performed only by the Indian women. Also, the travois poles appeared to be fastened under the riders' knees, instead of crossed over the ponies' necks. George Catlin made a similar mistake in one of his drawings, but there were no such errors in the hundreds of examples of Russell's work with which I was familiar. The three-initial signatures were not in Russell's usual style and furthermore were all in the lower right corner of the drawings instead of the lower left, where Russell almost invariably signed both his paintings and drawings. Finally, instead of the usual outline of a buffalo skull as a part of the signature, there was a tiny drawing of an Indian moccasin. In spite of these details there was such a feeling of life and originality about the sketches that I asked to take the book home for a

*A wedding picture: Charlie Russell and Nancy Cooper, 1896*
COLLECTION OF FREDERIC G. RENNER

few days, where I could examine it more carefully.

I had the portfolio for a week, and before the end of that time I was convinced that all of the drawings, crude as they were, had been done by Charles M. Russell and that this had been a boyhood sketchbook. The handwriting of the titles, misspelling and all, was also unquestionably his in my opinion. The word *Burlington* in flowing script on one page had obviously not been written by Charlie but was significant nevertheless. Charlie's last formal schooling had been in early 1880 at the age of fifteen when he attended one semester at a military school at Burlington, New Jersey. As his wife, Nancy Cooper Russell, later described his brief stay there: "He was made to walk guard for hours because book study was not in his mind. He would draw Indians, horses, or animals for any boy who would do his arithmetic in exchange." The old copybook had undoubtedly been Charlie's sketchbook at that time. The military academy at Burlington has long since passed out of existence, but it would be interesting, indeed, to know what books about Indians had been in the school library. One of Charlie's drawings, "Crow Indians in Ware Dress," could only have been inspired by Karl Bodmer's "Dance Leader of the Hidatsa

Dog Society." Others have a Catlinesque quality that suggests that Charlie must have been familiar with books illustrated by Catlin as well as Bodmer.

Much as I longed to possess the sketchbook, I couldn't afford the price being asked for it, and it was returned to the Veerhoff Galleries. I tried to learn something of its history, but about the only information I could elicit was that it had come from a Washington, D.C., family, members of which had known Charlie from his boyhood. Two or three years later I heard that the sketchbook was being offered for sale in Los Angeles, and I eventually learned that it had been purchased by my good friends Robert and Margaret Warden of Great Falls, Montana. So these sketches are now in good hands in Charlie Russell's country.

Charlie Russell had never seen a Plains Indian, a cowboy, or a grizzly bear in their native habitats when these sketches were executed. Even at this early age they show his intense interest in the many facets of the West. They also reveal, as nothing else could, how far he had to go to perfect his skills; and when compared with his drawings of only a few years later, how well and how fast he progressed. It is these elements that mark the significance of the Warden collection of Russell sketches. ☆

Although Charlie Russell's boyhood drawings were crude, they clearly project his sense of excitement with western subjects. Twenty years later he had become not only the consummate artist of countless finished drawings and paintings, but the casual master who could decorate his letters to friends with sketches like the one below: quickly drawn but alive with genuine feeling for men and horses in motion.

# "New York is worth twenty Richmonds"

One day in late October of 1864, as the Civil War was moving into its final stages, eight young men in civilian clothes arrived in New York City from Toronto by train. Though they spoke with southern accents, they were quickly caught up in the swirl of the city's life, for there were thousands of Southerners in New York—businessmen and planters who had come north to protect their interests; families fleeing from ruin; and ex-Confederate soldiers, prisoners of war on parole, looking for a way to return home. If these eight men acted out of the ordinary at all, their behavior went unnoticed.

They were, in fact, Confederate officers, volunteers in a desperate plot to force the North to accept southern independence in return for peace. The story of how close they came to succeeding underscores a major dread of any nation at war within itself: sabotage by an enemy who looks and acts like a friend.

Earlier that year, in the spring, Jefferson Davis had charged three men with carrying out Confederate designs from across the Union's weakest frontier, the more than one-thousand-mile border with Canada. Heading the mission was Colonel Jacob Thompson, a former aide to General P. G. T. Beauregard. A well-to-do Mississippian, Thompson

Gloating sinisterly, a Confederate arsonist prepares to set fire to a hotel room. Such a scene was witnessed at the Tammany Hotel.

*Harper's Weekly*, DEC. 17, 1864

before the war had been a congressman and Secretary of the Interior in Buchanan's Cabinet.

Canada was decidedly pro-Southern, although officially neutral. Toronto, where Thompson made his headquarters, was full of southern refugees—Kentuckians, Missourians, Marylanders, and Virginians especially. The city was also the roosting nest of spies and informers. "The bane and curse of carrying out anything in this country is the surveillance under which we act," Thomp-

son complained in a letter to Confederate Secretary of State Judah P. Benjamin. "Detectives or those ready to give information stand at every street corner. Two or three can not interchange ideas without a reporter." He warned against "any stranger who might claim an acquaintance, etc., as a swarm of detectives from the United States, male and female, [are] quartered in Toronto."

Thompson nevertheless plotted on, convinced that "nothing but violence can terminate the war." The result was a series of ill-conceived exploits, ail divulged in advance by informers at his elbow or spies behind his back. An elaborate scheme to promote a Northwest Confederacy was attempted in conjunction with Northern Copperheads, so-called "Peace" Democrats—and fizzled. Raids on Maine, the seizure of ships on the Great Lakes, the freeing of thousands of Confederate officers imprisoned at Johnson's Island in Lake Erie, an uprising in Chicago timed to coincide with the Democratic National Convention, a financial crisis to be brought on by pushing up the price of gold—not one scheme succeeded. Worse still, a minor raid on St. Albans, Vermont, caused such a furor that Canada soon became a questionable port of refuge. [See "The Hit-and-run Raid," AMERICAN

*By* NAT BRANDT

# In a last-ditch attempt to stave off defeat, the Confederate government in 1864 set in motion a startling plan of destruction

HERITAGE, August 1961.]

Something approaching madness seemed to infect the schemes and the schemers. Surprisingly, Thompson was undeterred by the timidity shown by the Copperheads in the Midwest and grew no more cautious regarding his confidants despite the disclosures that stymied every operation. If anything, he was more determined than ever to succeed by the fall of 1864, for the war was going badly—Sheridan was devastating the Shenandoah Valley, and Sherman had seized Atlanta. Then, on October 15, an editorial appeared in the Richmond *Whig* and was reprinted in its entirety by the *New-York Times*. It said, in part:

Sheridan reports to Grant that, in moving down the Valley to Woodstock, he has burned over two thousand barns filled with wheat, hay and farming implements, and over seventy mills filled with flour and wheat. . . . There is one effectual way, and only one that we know of, to arrest and prevent this and every other sort of atrocity —and that is to burn one of the chief cities of the enemy . . . and let its fate hang over the others as a warning of what may be done, and will be done to them, if the present system of war on the part of the enemy is continued. . . . New York is worth twenty Richmonds. . . .

Whether this was a signal from Richmond has never been determined. The idea of setting fire to

*Three principals in the plot to burn the city: top, bewhiskered Jacob Thompson and Robert M. Martin and, below, John W. Headley*
THE NEW-YORK HISTORICAL SOCIETY

New York and other northern cities had been considered for some time; the forthcoming Presidential election in the North, scheduled for November 8, provided the catalyst.

It was an ambitious plot. A small force of Confederate officers, smuggled into New York, was to set off a series of fires on Election Day as a diversion while Copperheads seized federal buildings and municipal offices, took control of the police department, freed prisoners from Fort Lafayette in New York Harbor, and

threw the Army commander in New York, Major General John Adams Dix, into a dungeon. By sunset the Confederate flag would fly over City Hall. Following the success of the "revolution," a convention of delegates from New York, New Jersey, and the New England states, where other insurrections were to be held, would be staged in New York to form a confederacy to cooperate with the government in Richmond.

The plan appeared valid to Thompson. New York was a Copperhead city, its politics feeding on the downtrodden and the corrupt, its philosophy a mixture of states' rights, appeasement, and outright support for the South. More than seven hundred thousand persons lived in the city, and they rejected Lincoln in 1860 by a two-to-one vote and would do so again.

The draft riots of July, 1863, had indicated how easily the embittered lower classes could be incited to riot and how ineffectual were New York's small police force and the token federal detachment stationed there. Moreover, fire fighting was in the hands of 125 volunteer companies whose members seemed more interested in racing each other than in putting out blazes; they insisted on dragging their cumbersome equipment through the streets by hand instead of using horses.

Of vital importance to the Confederates was the existence in New York of an active ring of Copperheads of considerable power and influence. Prominent among them were the two Wood brothers, both congressmen who would later vote against the Thirteenth Amendment, which abolished slavery. Before the war they had run a lottery in Louisiana. Fernando Wood, the older of the two and one-time mayor of New York, was an immaculately dressed, poker-faced corrupter who had risen to power on the shoulders of "twopenny" politicians; as mayor he had suggested, after the fall of Fort Sumter, that the city should secede from the Union. His brother Benjamin was publisher of one of the most virulent of anti-Lincoln newspapers, the *Daily News*, which had been instrumental in fanning the hatred that led to the draft riots.

There were others who were considered trustworthy, too: James A. McMaster, editor and publisher of the weekly *Freeman's Journal and Catholic Register;* Representative James Brooks, co-owner of the *Evening Express;* Rushmore G. Horton, editor of the *Weekly Day-Book;* and Hiram Cranston, proprietor of the New-York Hotel. In addition, it was believed that Governor Horatio Seymour, an opponent of abolition and the draft, might aid the plan.

The leader of the small Confederate band being sent to New York was Colonel Robert M. Martin of Kentucky. He and a fellow Kentuckian, Lieutenant John W. Headley, had served with the famed raider John Hunt Morgan. They had been sent by Richmond to Toronto that September to aid in military operations against the North. Martin, in his mid-twenties, had steel blue eyes and wore a mustache and goatee. He was six feet tall but walked slightly bent over because of a bullet wound in his right lung. Headley, whose memoirs were later to disclose the details of their exploits together, was known as Martin's boyish-looking

"assistant adjutant general."

Besides Martin and Headley the group included Captain Robert Kennedy. Kennedy, a profane, hard-drinking Louisianian, had recently escaped from the military prison on Johnson's Island; he had been wounded in the thigh during the Battle of Shiloh two years earlier and walked with a pronounced limp. All the others in the Confederate force were lieutenants—John T. Ashbrook, James T. Harrington, and James Chenault of Kentucky, John M. Price of Virginia, and a fifth whose name is unknown.

Greek fire was to be used. This was a mixture of phosphorus in a bi-sulfide of carbon that was commonly used in hand grenades, supposedly igniting spontaneously on contact with the air. It had been employed in an attack on shipping at St. Louis and in the St. Albans raid, though both times with unsatisfactory results. A Captain E. Longmire of Missouri was already in New York arranging for a supply of Greek fire when the eight Confederates, all in civilian clothes, boarded a train in Toronto in the last week of October. Each carried false papers.

After the Rebels arrived in New York, they immediately dispersed among several hotels and boarding houses to avoid suspicion. On Friday, October 28, with the national elections only ten days away, Martin, Headley, and Kennedy went to the *Freeman's Journal* to make contact with their Copperhead liaison, McMaster. The publisher was a big man —six feet three—and his piercing eyes and deep voice suggested power. Encouraged by his boast that the Copperheads had enlisted "about twenty thousand" men and had already distributed smuggled-in arms, the Rebels assured him in turn of "open, bold, and unflinching action when the hour arrived for crucial duty."

Further meetings with McMaster

were held over the next five days. At one, a man he identified as Governor Seymour's private secretary appeared, bringing with him the assurance that the Governor would cooperate. Then, on Thursday, November 3, with only five days left before the election, the first inkling that federal agents had uncovered the conspiracy came to light. That afternoon City Hall made public a telegram from Secretary of State William H. Seward. Similar wires had been sent to the mayors of thirteen other cities:

This Department has received information from the British Provinces to the effect that there is a conspiracy on foot to set fire to the principal cities in the Northern States on the day of the Presidential election. It is my duty to communicate this information to you.

The Copperheads grew more apprehensive of continuing in the plot when Major General Benjamin F. Butler arrived in the city the next day leading several thousand troops who had been hurriedly transferred from the front lines in Virginia. As Election Day neared, Butler set up a cordon around Manhattan. Two commandeered ferryboats filled with infantrymen were stationed in the Hudson River, another two in the East River. Artillery batteries, with their horses in harness, were put on board a vessel on the Jersey side of the Hudson. Gunboats were stationed off the Battery to protect the federal buildings and the Arsenal downtown; one also patrolled High Bridge on the Harlem River, guarding the Cro-

*The chief business and residential areas of New York were imperilled by the Rebel incendiary attack, the scope of which is indicated on this 1864 map. Besides fires at the eleven hotels shown here, one was set at the New England Hotel, in the densely populated Bowery district northwest of City Hall Park. There was also a second fire on the Hudson River docks near the one shown, and one at a lumberyard.*

MAP: THE NEW-YORK HISTORICAL SOCIETY; HOTELS: *Frank Leslie's Illustrated Newspaper,* DEC. 17, 1864

ST. JAMES HOTEL

FIFTH-AVENUE HOTEL

LA FARGE HOUSE

METROPOLITAN HOTEL

ST. NICHOLAS HOTEL

TAMMANY HOTEL

BARNUM'S MUSEUM

HUDSON RIVER DOCK

LOVEJOY'S HOTEL

ASTOR HOUSE

BELMONT HOTEL

HOWARD HOTEL

UNITED STATES HOTEL

ton Aqueduct link with the new reservoir in Central Park.

The Copperheads were thoroughly demoralized by the sudden turn in events. McMaster reported that only two others besides himself wanted to go ahead with the Election Day uprising. Accordingly, it was decided to postpone any action until Butler and his troops had left the city, after Election Day. As the days went by, the Copperheads grew even more reluctant to proceed. Martin pressed McMaster to set a new date, Thanksgiving Day, November 24. Before McMaster could return with an answer, the question was settled by General William Tecumseh Sherman, who set out with sixty thousand troops from Atlanta in mid-November, leaving that city in ruins, his destination unknown. On hearing the news McMaster and his colleagues immediately withdrew from any further connection with the conspiracy, arguing that it was doomed to failure. Two of the Confederate officers—Price and the one whose name is unknown—also backed out and returned to Canada. Longmire, the Missourian who had arranged with a chemist for supplies of the combustibles, disappeared.

Despite these setbacks, Sherman's destruction of Atlanta only served to incense the six remaining Confederate officers. As Kennedy declared later: "We wanted to let the people of the North understand that there are two sides to this war & that they cant be rolling in wealth & comfort, while we at the South are bearing all the hardship & privations." Thompson in Toronto had been told "he could expect to hear from us in New York, no matter what might be done in other cities," Headley said. "He seemed to approve our determination and hoped for no more failures, and especially now when our last card was to be played."

The Confederates laid their plans at a small cottage near Central Park loaned to them by a friend of Long-

mire's, a woman refugee from the South. From the start they decided to ignore federal and municipal buildings because they were guarded. The easiest places of access, as they had discovered in their wanderings around Manhattan, were the city's hotels. There were more than 125 of them, the most opulent on Broadway. The Astor House, across from City Hall Park, was the *grande dame* of them all; the largest hotel in the nation when it opened in 1836, it could accommodate four hundred guests. A little farther north on Broadway was the St. Nicholas Hotel, ideally situated near many theatres; built at a cost of more than one million dollars in 1854, the St. Nicholas was six stories tall and divided into three wings, with six hundred rooms that held upward of one thousand persons. Nearby, next door to Niblo's Garden, was the Metropolitan Hotel, which boasted thirteen thousand yards of carpeting and twelve miles of water and gas pipes; it handled six hundred lodgers with ease and had "sky parlors" from which lady guests could watch the promenade on Broadway below. A few blocks uptown was the marble-faced La Farge House, adjoining the Winter Garden Theatre; considered an "elegant resort" for the "floating population of the New World," the La Farge could accommodate more than five hundred persons.* Perhaps the most impressive hotel of all was the "new" Fifth-Avenue, which faced Madison Square, where Broadway came together with Fifth Avenue; it had rooms for eight hundred guests and a "perpendicular railway," an innovation especially popular with the elderly and with ladies.

Although other hotels throughout the city were less ostentatious, they were almost always busy, too, because of the comings and goings spurred by the war. Lovejoy's, on Park Row op-

*Of all the hotels, only the La Farge House still stands. Now called the Broadway Central Hotel, it has in recent years housed public-welfare recipients.

posite City Hall Park, catered to transient businessmen and travellers en route to other parts of the Union. The Tammany, a block away, was a favorite lunching spot for merchants. The United States, on Fulton Street near the East River, was a creaky but comfortable old hotel always filled with ship's captains. Businessmen in the Wall Street area lunched regularly at the Howard, one of the largest and best conducted of the older downtown hotels.

Each of the Confederates was assigned four hotels. Rooms were taken in advance when possible, under a variety of fictitious names. Meetings were held regularly at Headley's quarters, Room 204 at the Astor, where he had registered as "W. S. Haines." (Afterward the chambermaid would recall that the fireplace had been used unusually often to keep the room warm for his frequent visitors.) On Thanksgiving Day, November 24, as the North rejoiced over the prospect of victory over the South, Headley, acting on instructions left by Longmire, went to the chemist's basement shop in Greenwich Village and collected a suitcase filled with dozens of vials of a colorless liquid, the Greek fire.

The date now fixed for carrying out the plot was the next day, Friday. Like Thanksgiving, it also was a holiday in New York—Evacuation Day, celebrating the departure of the last British troops from the city after the Revolution. Barnum's Museum had scheduled an extra performance of the London drama *Waiting for the Verdict* in anticipation of large holiday crowds. The Booth brothers—Edwin, Junius Brutus, and John Wilkes—were to appear together for the first time in *Julius Caesar* at the Winter Garden in a benefit performance to raise money for a statue of Shakespeare to be erected in Central Park. Niblo's Garden was featuring William Wheatley in the new rave melodrama *The Corsican Brothers*.

The Confederates planned to start the fires from 8 P.M. onward. The arson, they decided, would be confined chiefly to the business districts, but Headley was also to set several fires along the wharves of the Hudson to confuse the fire department and to destroy valuable cargoes.

By six o'clock Friday evening, when the Rebels met for the last time, most of them had booked rooms at several of their assigned hotels. The rest of the rooms were to be taken that night, as the men circulated about the city. Each was instructed to pile all the bedding and the mattress atop the bed and then to douse the heap with the Greek fire. To avoid detection windows, shutters, and doors were to be shut tight while they worked, and the doors carefully closed upon leaving. As the Rebels packed the vials of Greek fire into cheap black carpet-bags, Martin appeared in the uniform of a federal officer; he had brought it from Toronto in a trunk.

The first fire alarm sounded from the St. James Hotel, at Broadway and Twenty-sixth Street, at 8:43 P.M. A guest in Room 85, on the topmost floor, smelled a peculiar odor. On opening his door he found the hallway full of smoke. He ran down the stairs calling for help. Within minutes the second alarm was sounded at the St. Nicholas Hotel, at Broadway and Spring Street, when a guest saw smoke coming from under the door to Room 174.

Instead of the customary nine o'clock all-clear gong, the watchman at the City Hall fire tower was repeatedly plunging the lever that rang the enormous twenty-three-thousand-pound bell: one ring for the First Fire District, a pause, four rings for the Fourth Fire District, a pause; then the cycle was repeated over and over again. The tolling was picked up by watchmen at the other fire towers in the city. Soon they interspersed eight rings for the Eighth Fire District.

The alarm from the Eighth Fire

*The only Confederate caught and tried, Captain Robert C. Kennedy, was photographed three days before he was hanged.*
COLLECTION OF THE AUTHOR

District was sounded at Barnum's Museum, located on Broadway at Ann Street. Kennedy had made an unscheduled stop there, going upstairs into the building to see from a window in the stairwell whether any fires had taken hold. Upon hearing the first alarm he returned to the street outside and headed for his next assignment. As he went downstairs, he flung a vial of phosphorus back at the stairs "just to scare the people." Soon afterward, an usher ran out of the building, crying "Fire!" In the Lecture-Room on the fifth floor panic had already seized the audience and members of the cast of *Waiting for the Verdict.* Cries of "Fire! Fire!" came from every side. Several people slid down the pillars from the gallery to the parquet. Women and children shrieked with fear. As men fought to get by them to the exits, several women fainted. The alarm spread to the floors below, too. Barnum's seven-foot-tall giantess, her hair flying wildly behind her, lurched down the stairs and out an exit. Turning the corner, she ran down Ann

Street and straight into a saloon. Those who reached the street behind her burst out of the museum in a virtual stampede.

Meanwhile, uptown at the La Farge House the servant girl stationed on the third floor passed by Room 104 and saw, through the transom above the door, a light in the room. Its occupant had left a few minutes earlier. Believing he had left the gaslight on by mistake—he had made such a fuss looking for matches to light it—she stopped by the door and was about to open it when a burst of flame suddenly lit up the hallway.

Next door, the second act of *Julius Caesar* was in progress at the Winter Garden Theatre when someone apparently whispered to a companion, "The La Farge is on fire." Others nearby heard only the last word— "Fire." Soon it was being repeated throughout the audience. Several women in the dress circle stood up. When they did, almost the entire audience, from parquet to dome, followed their example. Onstage the play stopped. Edwin Booth broke off his lines to race to the wings. He returned to the stage a few minutes later. Standing in the center by the footlights, his arms outstretched, he pleaded for order. But many persons were already at the doors, pushing and shoving to get out.

It was shortly after ten o'clock when the cry of "Fire" ran through the Metropolitan Hotel, on Broadway at Prince Street. At Niblo's Garden adjoining it two actors were duelling back and forth across the stage in the dramatic last act of *The Corsican Brothers.* Someone in the gallery suddenly shouted "Fire!" The audience rose as one to its feet. Women began hoisting their skirts and leaping from chair to chair as they made for the doors. Up in the balcony men tried to hold back others from throwing themselves down to the parquet below. Those nearest exits were already rushing through them.

The pattern seemed clear as midnight approached. Hotels, theatres, and docks—uptown, downtown, from the Hudson to the East River—were being set afire en masse. Shock waves of fear fanned the excitement in the streets. Would-be looters in droves from the grim sections that girded the heart of the city swarmed around the scenes of the alarms, so many appearing so quickly that at first the fires were blamed on them. Then another rumor spread along Broadway—a Confederate attack.

As detachments of police struggled to keep order, new alarms rang through the chill night, sending volunteer firemen scurrying to answer the calls for help. A roundsman from the Second Precinct spotted flames in an upper-story window of the United States Hotel at Fulton and Water streets. Ten blocks north, near the heart of the Bowery, the staff of the New England Hotel, alerted to the possibility of trouble, was checking each room; when the door to Number 58 was opened, a sheet of flame shot out.

A half mile away, on Park Row overlooking City Hall, a guest going up to his room on the fourth floor of Lovejoy's Hotel saw smoke issuing from under the door of Room 121. At the same time, along the Hudson, a police officer and a dozen sailors were pouring water on the flaming bales of hay stacked on a bulkhead opposite North Moore and Beach streets.

The next alarm came from across town—at Fulton Street again, this time just off Broadway at the Belmont Hotel next door to the Herald Building. The source of the acrid smoke was Room 28 on the second floor; the room, the hotel clerk later remembered, had been taken earlier that night by an Army officer.

A few short blocks away the porter and the bookkeeper of French's Hotel stood transfixed, looking out from the window of the porter's attic room. Directly across narrow Frankfort Street, which separated French's from the Tammany Hotel, they could see a man having trouble, so it appeared, starting a fire with matches in the middle of the room. It was Kennedy; fortified by several drinks, he had evidently forgotten to close the shutters and apparently had decided not to let the phosphorus do its work unassisted. The porter and the bookkeeper raced downstairs and into the street. Outside, along Park Row, volunteer firemen of Peterson Engine Company Number 31 were hauling their pumper, "The White Ghost," back to its post in densely populated Chrystie Street. On hearing the porter's cries for help they immediately pulled the pumper into Frankfort Street and began laying hose. Frank Mahedy, the foreman, raced ahead into the Tammany Hotel; he soon emerged with a drowsy young girl in his arms. Then he ran back inside again, this time returning with the girl's mother. Both had been asleep in the room next to the one that the porter and the bookkeeper had seen being set on fire. In the excitement Kennedy slipped away unnoticed.

It was 2:30 in the morning when a house detective opened the door of Room 148 in the Fifth-Avenue Hotel. He was greeted by a rush of smoke. Several miles away on Broadway, in the Howard Hotel at Maiden Lane, the guest in the room next to Number 44 was roused from his sleep when smoke began to fill his room. Meanwhile, the sailors who had put out the fire on the wharf by the Hudson River were out again in the chill night. This time they were fighting a fire aboard the barge *Merchant*; it was berthed only a block away from the site of the earlier fire. And as dawn came up, two workmen at a lumberyard at nearby West and Clarkson streets found stacks of wood beams and the hay in adjacent stables smoldering when they came to work.

Almost twelve hours after the first alarm, the last was sounded. At about nine o'clock on Saturday morning, a smoldering fire was discovered in Room 204, on the fourth floor of the Astor House, on Broadway across from Barnum's Museum, during a room-by-room inspection by hotel personnel.

By then it was clear that the city had been spared from a major disaster by dozens of instances of good luck. Only Headley and Kennedy appeared to have fulfilled their assignments; instead of fires in twenty-four hotels only twelve had been set, and servants or guests had detected the fires before they had gotten out of control. In some hotels, as on the docks, the phosphorus had smoldered for hours, causing in most cases a great deal of smoke but little else. Headley later blamed both Longmire and the chemist who had provided the Greek fire, but the truth was that he and the other Confederates had unwittingly blundered. As Fire Marshal Alfred E. Baker reported after testing the contents of some vials that were discarded in haste at several hotels:

The chemist had done his work sagaciously, but in carrying out the plan a blunder was committed which defeated the anticipated results. In each case the doors and windows of the room were left closed, so that when the phosphorous ignited, the fire only smouldered from the want of oxygen necessary to give it activity, thus affording an opportunity for its detection before much harm was done.... Happily, as I have shown, this fiendish plan was defeated by one of those miscalculations which so often interpose to frustrate the designs of evil-minded men....

No lives were lost, no one—amazingly—seriously injured, despite the panics at Barnum's and the theatres. The volunteer fire companies, to everyone's further surprise, had behaved meritoriously. The most damage incurred was at the St. Nicholas Hotel; it cost ten thousand

CONTINUED ON PAGE 106

HIS GRANDSON RECALLS:

# The Life and Death of Thomas Nast

*To his contemporaries Thomas Nast was unquestionably America's greatest and most effective political cartoonist, attacking corruption with a brilliant and often vitriolic pen, harrying the bosses, creating the political symbols that still remain the emblems of our two major political parties. His grandson's impression is quite different. He remembers him as a gentle and witty companion, as the creator of our conception of Santa Claus, as a sad and lonely man whose life ended poignantly in a foreign land. Harper & Row, whose predecessor company first published in 1890 a collection of Nast's Christmas pictures, will reprint later this month* Thomas Nast's Christmas Drawings for the Human Race, *with a new text by that grandson, Thomas Nast St. Hill. The following article is excerpted from this biographical reminiscence.*

## By THOMAS NAST ST. HILL

**AMERICAN HERITAGE BOOK SELECTION**

Th. Nast: His Period and His
Pictures, BY ALBERT BIGELOW PAINE
(MACMILLAN, 1904)

*Either overtly as subjects or anonymously as models, Thomas Nast often used himself or members of his family in his cartoons. At top is a caricature of himself at fifteen asking Frank Leslie for a job. The elegant lady with the flowery hat is Dame Fashion, demanding an end to the slaughter of birds for hat trimmings. She looks, however, suspiciously like Nast's wife, Sarah.*

COLLECTION OF THE AUTHOR

M y grandfather Thomas Nast, America's most famous political cartoonist and the creator of the image of Santa Claus as we recognize him today, was born in 1840 in a military barracks in Landau, Bavaria, where his father was a musician in the 9th Regiment Bavarian Band. The elder Nast, my great-grandfather, while not an agitator, was a man of liberal ideas; and in view of the political turmoil then prevalent in Germany his friendly commandant suggested that America might be a better place for a man so fond of free speech. So it was that my grandfather, then six years old, and his mother and older sister departed for the United States in 1846 and settled in New York. Nast senior followed four years later after serving out his enlistment. Upon his arrival in New York he found employment in the orchestra of Burton's Theatre on Chambers Street and became a member of the Philharmonic Society.

As soon as they were settled in New York, Thomas and his older sister were entered in one of the city's public schools. The young German boy was handicapped by not being able to speak a word of English. Furthermore, it soon became apparent that my grandfather was no scholar. His only interest was in drawing, and after six years of regular schooling his parents decided to transfer him to art school. Here he proved an apt pupil, but his father found that the tuition was prohibitive on a musician's wages. Consequently, at age fifteen Thomas Nast's formal education was abruptly ended, and he went out into the world to earn his living. Surprisingly, he was offered a job following his first interview.

When the roly-poly German boy appeared in the office of *Frank Leslie's Illustrated Newspaper*, a popular weekly published in New York, he was ushered into the presence of publisher Frank Leslie, to whom he showed some of his sketches and explained that he would like to draw for the magazine. Seeking to impress the aspiring fifteen-year-old with the absurdity of his request, Leslie gave him an assignment. It was to go down to the Christopher Street ferry-house in lower Manhattan during the rush hour and draw a picture of the crowd boarding the boat. To the publisher's great surprise the young artist returned with a very commendable picture that won him a job as illustrator with *Leslie's* at a salary of four dollars a week. For several years thereafter Nast's drawings appeared in the magazine, and it was during this time that he drew his first cartoons attacking civic dishonesty.

It was fortunate that my grandfather went to work when he did, for in 1858 his father died, and the artist, then eighteen, was obliged to contribute to the support of his mother. Not long afterward *Leslie's* was forced to cut salaries because of financial problems, and young Nast left the magazine and went to work in a friend's art studio. While there he made his first drawing for *Harper's Weekly*, and in 1859 a page of his pictures depicting the police scandal in New York City was accepted by the magazine.

During these years young Thomas met and fell in love with Sarah Edwards, a cultured and charming young lady of English parentage, who would later become his wife— and my grandmother. Although his wages had increased to twenty dollars a week, Nast was hardly in a position to ask Miss Edwards' hand in marriage. Accordingly, when an offer came to join the staff of the *New York Illustrated News* at twice his current salary, he jumped at it.

Next came an opportunity to go abroad for the *News* and send back pictures of the Heenan-Sayers heavyweight championship fight in England. Nast accepted the assignment, hoping that by so doing he could acquire the necessary nest egg on which to get married.

In February, 1860, the artist, not yet twenty years old, sailed for England, very much in love, as his letters home revealed, but not quite sure that his Sally would be waiting for him when he returned.

Thomas Nast's trip abroad lasted a year and included a stint in Italy covering Giuseppe Garibaldi's campaign to liberate his native country from Austrian domination. When Nast arrived home, he had hardly improved his fortunes. In fact, he had only a dollar and a half in his pocket. But Sally was still waiting faithfully for him, and he was no longer deterred from pressing his suit.

He went back to work for the *News* and finally prevailed upon Sally's parents to consent to their marriage, which took place on September 26, 1861, the day before Thomas Nast's twenty-first birthday. The bride was twenty.

Earlier that year, when the Civil War had broken out, my grandfather had considered enlisting; but those who knew of his talents convinced him that he could better serve his country with his pencil than with a sword. Thus it was that the young bridegroom began covering the Civil War for *Harper's Weekly*. Then in July, 1863, he went to the front as artist on the scene for that magazine. His Civil War drawings attracted nationwide attention, and the young artist's reputation grew.

For the 1862 Christmas issue of *Harper's Weekly* Nast drew a picture of Santa Claus, inspired by a poem composed forty years earlier by Clement Clarke Moore. Professor Moore had made up "A Visit from Saint Nicholas" for the amusement of his six small children and hadn't even thought of publishing it. But his wife had recorded the poem in the family Bible; subsequently it had

*This detail of an 1863 picture showing Union soldiers giving food to starving civilians is typical of Nast's deeply stirring Civil War drawings.*
*Harper's Weekly, JAN. 17, 1863*

made its way into print. Nast apparently read the poem sometime in 1862 and drew Santa Claus, with sleigh and reindeer, much as Moore had described him.

This Christmas drawing marks the first appearance of Santa Claus as we know him today. So it may be said that Clement Clarke Moore, a learned American professor of Biblical languages, and Thomas Nast, a young German-born artist, gave the world a new image of St. Nicholas and one that would live in the hearts of children for generations to come.

Thomas Nast covered the Civil War for *Harper's* for its entire duration, and his cartoons so stirred the hearts of Northerners that President Lincoln referred to him as the Union's best recruiting sergeant. When the fighting was over, General Grant was to say that Thomas Nast had done as much as any one man to preserve the Union and bring the war to an end, a remarkable tribute to the young cartoonist.

Nast's relationship with *Harper's* was firmly established by 1865, and in the twenty years to follow, the magazine and the artist would become champions of honesty in government and bulwarks of Republicanism.

In 1870 Nast launched an attack on New York's corrupt Tweed Ring. While his campaign against Boss Tweed is familiar to students of American history, it is less well known that in 1871 my grandfather refused a bribe of a half million dollars to call off his attacks and go abroad to study art. Tweed did not so much mind what the papers printed about him, he said, because most of his constituents couldn't read but they could see "them damn pictures."

Failing in its attempt to bribe Nast, the Tweed Ring next threatened the publisher of *Harper's* by throwing all of the company's textbooks out of the city schools and ordering the Tweed-controlled board of education to re-

ject all future Harper & Brothers bids for school books. *Harper's* board of directors almost capitulated, but Nast's loyal friend Fletcher Harper stood by him and the fight went on. Nast continued his campaign against the Ring despite threats against his life, vowing that he would see them all in jail before he stopped. When suspicious-looking characters were observed loitering about his home in upper Manhattan and the friendly police captain in the neighborhood was suddenly transferred to another precinct, Nast decided that it was time to move his family out of the city. It was at this time that he bought Villa Fontana in suburban

Morristown, New Jersey, which was to be my grandparents' home for the next thirty years.

Thomas Nast's cartoon *The Tammany Tiger Loose*, which appeared as a double-page spread in *Harper's* just before the fall elections in 1871, is considered one of the most powerful cartoons of all time and was principally responsible for the defeat of the Tweed Ring at the polls a few days later. It was printed from a wood engraving, and all of Tweed's gang are clearly identifiable.

After being prosecuted for having looted the city of over thirty million dollars in the course of thirty months, members of the Ring were jailed, but

THE AMERICAN RIVER

Although raised a Catholic, Nast drew some viciously anticlerical cartoons. *In* The American River Ganges, *below, he shows the prelates of the Church as crocodiles, protecting the Catholic fortress Tammany Hall and attacking American schoolchildren. The issue was public versus parochial schools. After this cartoon appeared in* Harper's Weekly *for September 30, 1871, the magazine felt called upon to explain that Nast was not anti-Church but only opposed the Catholics when they dabbled in politics and tried to undermine the principle of separation of church and state. Boss Tweed, shown as a vulture on page 81, is here depicted as a bloated giant.* Can the law reach him?—The dwarf and the giant thief *was Nast's caption for this one.* Communism (below) *reminded Nast of the slaughter at the Paris Commune and appears as a deathly revolutionist in the cockade of the Terror. His ironic caption reads,* The Emancipator of Labor and the Honest Working-People.

Harper's Weekly, JAN. 6, 1872

GANGES.

Harper's Weekly, FEB. 7, 1874

*"Hello! Santa Claus!"*

*With pipe in hand, a jolly, bearded Santa Claus, opposite, as created by Thomas Nast, receives a very up-to-date communication—a long-distance telephone call.*
BOTH: *Christmas Drawings for the Human Race* (HARPER & BROS., 1890)

Tweed himself managed to escape to Europe. There he was captured and returned to the United States. Ironically Tweed was apprehended in Spain on a charge of kidnapping, though this was one crime of which he had never been guilty. Authorities in this country, at a loss to understand the charge, later learned that Tweed had been recognized from a Nast cartoon that showed Tweed in prison garb with two little ragamuffins in tow. This was a cartoon that my grandfather had drawn some years earlier to illustrate Tweed's expressed willingness, when seeking the governorship of New York State, to bring all manner of minor thieves to justice.

When Tweed died in New York City's Ludlow Street Jail in 1878, every one of Nast's cartoons attacking him was found among his effects.

Thomas Nast's part in overthrowing the Tweed Ring added to the na-tionwide prominence he had gained during the war. He had become a political power, every Presidential candidate that he supported having been elected. Even General Grant, upon assuming the Presidency, attributed his election to the "sword of Sheridan and the pencil of Thomas Nast."

The symbols that Nast originated during this period were to outlive their creator. Between 1870 and 1874 the Republican elephant and the Democratic donkey made their first appearances. Both were conceptions of Thomas Nast, based on the fables of Aesop. Today's familiar images of Uncle Sam, John Bull, and Columbia also were conceived by Nast during this period.

My grandfather was a controversial character. Whereas the staunchly Republican Union League Club of New York honored him for his ardent devotion to the preservation of the Union, the New York *World* in 1867 accused him of bigotry and pandering to the "meanest passions and prejudices of the most unthoughtful persons of the day." To Nast all things were either black or white. There was nothing in between. He was absolutely merciless in his attacks upon those with whom he disagreed. The Ku Klux Klan, anarchists, Communists, corrupt politicians, and even the Irish and the Catholic Church were among those upon whom he vented his wrath. Obviously one's opinion of the artist depended largely upon whether one agreed with his views or not.

By 1877 my grandfather was a relatively wealthy man with an unusually good income in terms of that day. Not yet forty years old, he had just about everything that he could wish for—a nationwide reputation for integrity, a lovely home, a devoted wife and family, and financial independence. Sarah Nast had contributed greatly to her husband's success. She regularly read to him as he worked. Shakespeare and the Bible were the inspirations for many of the artist's drawings, and Sarah Nast often supplied the ideas and captions for them. My grandmother was a charming hostess and entertained her husband's distinguished friends graciously and unostentatiously. General Grant and his wife and Mark Twain were guests on more than one occasion.

As the result of his national prominence the artist frequently received offers to lecture, few of which he accepted. It was an activity that he cordially disliked. For one thing it kept him away from his home, where he now did all of his work. Equally important was the fact that he suffered so acutely from stage fright that he often became ill before an appearance.

Some offers were hard to refuse, such as one extended by the Boston Lyceum Bureau offering ten thousand dollars for a ten-week tour. But at the time the artist was too busy with his assignments for *Harper's*, work that he much preferred. Two years later he was approached again, with an offer of "a larger sum for a hundred lectures than any man living." But Nast again declined.

In 1877, Mark Twain, Granddad's good friend, proposed in a letter a plan that must have been very tempting:

My Dear Nast:
I did not think I should ever stand on a platform again until the time was come for me to say "I die innocent." But the same old offers keep arriving. I have declined them all, just as usual, though sorely tempted, as usual.

Now, I do not decline because I mind talking to an audience, but because (1) travelling alone is so heart-breakingly dreary, and (2) shouldering the whole show is such a cheer-killing responsibility.

Therefore, I now propose to you what you proposed to me in November, 1867, ten years ago (when I was unknown), viz., that you stand on the platform and make pictures, and I stand by you and blackguard the audience. I should enormously enjoy meandering around (to big towns—I don't want to go to the little ones) with you for company.

My idea is not to fatten the lecture agents and lyceums on the spoils, but put all the ducats religiously into two equal piles, and say to the artist and lecturer, "Absorb these." . . .

Call the gross receipts $100,000 for four months and a half, and the profit from $60,000 to $75,000 (I try to make the figures large enough and leave it to the public to reduce them).

I did not put in Philadelphia because P_____ owns that town, and last winter when I made a little reading-trip he only paid me $300 and pretended his concert (I read fifteen minutes in the midst of a concert) cost him a vast sum, and so he couldn't afford any more. I could get up a better concert with a barrel of cats. . . .

Well, you think it over, Nast, and drop me a line. We should have some fun.
Yours truly,
Samuel L. Clemens.

It seemed a fascinating plan, but again my grandfather had no inclination to leave his home and family, and so he again regretted.

By 1879 Thomas Nast was beginning to get restive. Changes in management at *Harper's* had resulted in less freedom to express his own views. A new generation of publishers did not wholly agree with what they considered their artist's tendency to advocate startling and, in their opinion, sometimes radical reforms. Then, too, with the introduction of new techniques in reproduction, the hand-engraved woodblock, which Nast had used to such advantage, had become outmoded and the new methods were less suited to his style. Consequently, as Nast's drawings appeared less frequently in the *Weekly*, he took advantage of the opportunity to travel and invest his savings. While my grandfather would have been the last to realize it, he had, at the age of thirty-nine, reached his peak.

Nast had learned little about finance during his career as an artist,

as would soon become apparent. An investment in a silver mine in Colorado proved unprofitable and became a drain on his resources. But in 1883 his financial problems seemed about to be over. His good friend General U. S. Grant had, after retiring from the Presidency, invested all of his savings in a Wall Street firm headed by Ferdinand Ward, a New York investment banker. Grant's son, who lacked financial experience, was made a junior partner to look after his father's interest. The venture prospered to such an extent, or so it appeared, that General Grant offered Nast an opportunity to participate, a privilege accorded only to a select few. This seemed the chance to recoup his mining losses, so the artist sold a piece of property and invested the proceeds in the firm of Grant and Ward. The generous dividends that ensued encouraged Nast to take his family abroad for a much-needed rest.

It was not long after his return, however, that headlines in his morning paper announced that Grant and Ward had failed. It seemed incredible in view of the optimistic reports and liberal dividends he had been receiving. But the fact was that Ferdinand Ward had proved to be an unscrupulous manipulator who, in order to maintain the fiction of profitability, had been declaring dividends out of capital funds until there was no more capital left.

My grandfather lost everything that he had invested, while General Grant lost even more. Grant had personally guaranteed one of the firm's notes a few days before the failure was announced and, in order to help pay off the note, had to sell everything he could get his hands on, including military trophies and souvenirs from all over the world. Not until Grant's memoirs were published posthumously was his family able to pay off all of the General's debts.

The disenchantment that followed Nast's first and final experience in Wall Street was revealed in several of his pictures. One, a merciless and funny self-caricature in oil painted eighteen years later, depicts the artist's complete bewilderment and despair at being duped. (This painting, on loan from the Smithsonian Institution, hung in the White House office of Daniel P. Moynihan during the time he served as a counsellor to President Nixon. It was known among Dr. Moynihan's colleagues as *Nast Contemplating the "Bust" of Ward*.)

Relations between Nast and *Harper's* did not improve during the Presidential campaign of 1884, when the cartoonist found himself unable to support James G. Blaine, the Republican candidate for the Presidency. For the first time Thomas Nast campaigned for a Democrat, caricaturing Blaine as the "Plumed Knight." Grover Cleveland, the Democratic candidate whom Nast supported, was elected.

In 1886 came the end of Thomas

*"Hello! Little One!"*

Nast's association with *Harper's Weekly*, a magazine that he had helped make famous and in which he had made his reputation. In the quarter century of the Nast-*Harper's* relationship the nation had passed through a turbulent period, and Nast's drawings in the magazine would provide a vivid pictorial chronicle of those years. But in terminating his connection with *Harper's* Nast lost his forum, while at the same time the *Weekly* lost its political importance.

Several years later my grandfather tried starting his own paper, but this venture, too, failed, leaving the artist heavily in debt. Nast consoled himself, however, that he had lost no one's money but his own. Now came the time when horses and carriages had to be sold, faithful servants dismissed, and a mortgage placed on the house.

It was like manna from heaven, therefore, when in 1889 his old friends at *Harper's* proposed that he get together a collection of his Christmas drawings for publication in book form, a very Christmaslike gesture and one that my grandfather gratefully accepted.

Thomas Nast's book *Christmas Drawings for the Human Race* was published in time for the 1890 Christmas season. It contained pictures that had appeared in Christmas issues of *Harper's* over a period of thirty years as well as some additional drawings made especially for the book. Clement Moore's "A Visit from Saint Nicholas" was again the inspiration for many of the new Christmas drawings, and Santa Claus was now depicted as the very embodiment of merriment and good cheer.

It seemed fitting that Thomas Nast's last assignment for *Harper's* should be on a theme transcending the fortunes of politics, thus giving the artist an opportunity to include all humans in his message of Christmas good will, regardless of their race, creed, or political affiliation.

*The dreams of childhood are portrayed by Thomas Nast in* Christmas Drawings for the Human Race. *With Santa Claus and his reindeer right up front, dozens of familiar characters from children's literature climb, tumble, and swarm around the sleeping children.*

My earliest personal memories of my grandfather relate to the many times that I visited the Morristown home in the years just before and after the turn of the century. I was fortunate in being a favorite of his as a boy, no doubt because my mother, Edith Nast, was very close to her father and I was his eldest grandson.

Following the publication of his *Christmas Drawings for the Human Race* in 1890, my grandfather spent a great deal of his time in his studio at home, painting. He seemed to find peace and relaxation in quietly working on his canvases. The days of the crusading cartoonist who sometimes dipped his pen in vitriol were past. Thomas Nast, the painter, was a gentler person and the only one that this grandson ever knew.

Most of my grandfather's paintings had to do with Civil War subjects, many of them based on sketches he had made on the scene thirty years earlier. His huge canvas showing New York's famous 7th Regiment marching down Broadway on its way to war in April of 1861 and his *Peace in Union* painting depicting the surrender scene at Appomattox four years later have been widely reproduced and are recognized for their historical accuracy. In a different vein was his *Immortal Light of Genius*, a tribute to William Shakespeare, a replica of which hung in the Shakespeare Memorial at Stratford-on-Avon, England. It was stored during enemy bombing attacks in

*In 1898 Nast presented our author, Thomas Nast St. Hill, to a new Nast grandchild, his cousin Thomas Nast Crawford.*

World War II but was, unfortunately, irreparably damaged. Thomas Nast's *Head of Christ*, acquired by J. Pierpont Morgan, was loaned by Morgan to the Metropolitan Museum of Art, in New York City, where it was once shown.

Had Thomas Nast followed his early aspiration to become a painter, he might well have earned recognition in that field rather than as a cartoonist. As it was, his training was not such as to gain him the reputation in the field of art that he was to win in caricature. Critics have acknowledged that his paintings,

while they appear labored, have a heavy power and deserve more recognition than they have received.

Most of my grandfather's paintings were commissioned by old friends; and while payments were liberal, income from this source was insufficient to support his family.

During his painting years the artist often hung his paintings next to a large window to dry in the sun, sometimes upside-down or sideways. Included among these were his self-caricature and his head of Christ. On one occasion during this period the delivery of my grandfather's daily paper was suddenly discontinued. Upon complaining to the distributor, he learned that the young boy who used to deliver the papers had seen what he thought to be strange people looking out of the window. The paper boy concluded that the house was haunted; and when he finally saw the Lord himself peering out of the window, he was definitely through and would deliver no more papers to that house!

Of course, I was not old enough to appreciate that my grandfather was having financial problems; but I later learned that it distressed him that he was unable to be as generous to his family and friends as he had been during his more affluent years.

*Thomas Nast often communicated with his young grandson through pictures—swift, funny sketches designed to tickle a small child. He would often draw around St. Hill's youthful scribbles, adding a caricature of himself reacting to his grandson's "art." Note the "Budy," a misspelling of the author's boyhood nickname, in the sketch at right.*

I recall Thomas Nast as a relatively short man, perhaps five feet six or seven, always impeccably dressed in dark jacket with boutonniere, waistcoat with gold watch chain, a stickpin in his ascot tie, and gray striped trousers such as worn with a cutaway. He was very distinguished looking with his gray hair, which was always tousled, his Vandyke beard, and flowing mustaches. He wore a wide-brimmed fedora and carried a silver-headed cane, which he often tucked under his arm as he strode along. There was something of the actor in him, and he was, in fact, a member of The Players, a club in New York whose membership roster included most of the leading actors of the day, as well as some artists and musicians.

My grandfather took me to the club on several occasions, but I cannot say that I recall any of the stage celebrities I met there. Strange as it may seem, the character I most clearly recall from one of those visits was the traffic policeman at a busy intersection nearby. The officer tipped his helmet and greeted my grandfather by name as we crossed the street together, whereupon we stopped in the middle of the crowded thoroughfare as I was introduced. A very proud moment!

From time to time my grandfather took me to the theatre or circus in New York, and on one such occasion I recall going backstage to meet the famous actor Joseph Jefferson, who played Rip in *Rip Van Winkle*. I was

*The three drawings that record the author's first spree with his grandfather, as described in the text, are shown at right. The Cupid has a distinctly Nastian head.*

even more impressed that Buffalo Bill was a friend of my grandfather's. I can still recall the shooting of the cowboys and the yelping of the Indian warriors in Buffalo Bill's exciting Wild West show. And I remember seeing Annie Oakley shoot clay pigeons from every conceivable posture. The show was presented in Madison Square Garden, and I wondered why the bullets from Annie Oakley's gun didn't kill some of the audience, not realizing that she used a shotgun, not a rifle. Tickets to most of the performances we attended together were free passes, known at the time as Annie Oakleys because they had holes punched in them, as though perforated by Annie's shotgun.

Among the most treasured souvenirs of my relationship with my grandfather are three sketches commemorating our first spree together. I was seven years old at the time. The first of these, sent on Valentine's Day, 1902, announced in rhyme that we were to go on a spree the following Wednesday. My mother had arranged to provide the necessary funds for the outing. The next sketch, five days later, is a message that speaks for itself. It shows my grandfather sitting on the edge of his chair, hat on, cane in hand, ready and eager to be off. But the dollar sign and the question mark on his travelling bag tell the story. The check has not arrived! The problem was apparently solved before the big day, however, as the final sketch shows us marching joyfully down the street after attending a matinee at the Broadway Theatre. The description of our first spree as having been "done up Brown" refers to our luncheon at Brown's, a well-known chophouse for men in New York at the time.

That Thomas Nast was conscious

91

# AN ILLUSTRATED THANK-YOU NOTE

*After a visit in 1872 with President and Mrs. Grant, Nast returned home bearing gifts from his hosts for the children. The following sketches were included in his thank-you note, which began, "Dear Mr. and Mrs. General."*

*"The knife is a perfect success. Tom has been going around . . . stabbing people ever since he had it given to him, his young sister Edith in particular."*

*"Edith regards her medal as a most exact time keeper, carries it all around with her . . . gravely informing us at noon time that 'It is twenty-five of six.'"*

*"Julia's work basket gives her such pleasure, she meditates perpetrating a note of thanks on the subject . . ."*

*"The baby . . . manifests great intelligence for one of her tender age, expressing herself much pleased at my return."*

of his short stature is evidenced by the caricatures he sometimes drew of himself standing on something to give him height. In one such cartoon he showed himself on a chair delivering a speech. The occasion was a Canvasback Club dinner at Harvey's Restaurant in Washington, D.C. He had become separated from his baggage on the train and was obliged to appear in his business suit instead of white tie and tails. He made up for his unsuitable attire in the cartoon, however, which shows him in formal dress, with an apologetic caption that says: *How He Should Have Appeared.* This cartoon, together with one he drew of his host, the late George W. Harvey, still hangs on the wall of the famous Washington restaurant. Mr. Harvey once stated that he had several times refused offers of a thousand dollars for the drawings.

Other sketches that I prize highly reveal Thomas Nast's cleverness and sense of humor. Before I was old enough to write, I sometimes enclosed in my mother's letters to her father pictures that I had drawn myself. They showed no evidence that I had inherited any of the artist's talent. Several of my drawings were returned after "Pop Tom," as I called him, had worked them into sketches of his own, like one in which he made my drawing appear on an easel before which he stood appraising the work of his latest "Rival in the Art field." Others showing his shocked incredulity on viewing his grandson's art were similarly returned. And when I was unable to draw a fish, he made a sketch of a fish "drawing" me.

Thomas Nast's original sketches were highly valued by recipients, and they often took the place of formal correspondence. He blamed his reluctance to write on his pen, which he said did not know how to spell. He was a notoriously bad speller and sometimes mistakes crept into his captions, such as "Budy" for "Buddy," my childhood nickname, in the fish sketch. Fortunately Sarah Nast corrected most of his misspelled captions before they appeared.

I remember seeing my grandfather at work in his home studio. I recall particularly the three-foot-high bronze statue *The Gladiator* above his roll-top desk and his pet mockingbird in a cage close by. As I now realize, the statue of the gladiator was symbolic, in that it represented one who, like Thomas Nast himself, engaged in fierce combat or controversy. The studio was on the second floor; and when the mockingbird heard his master's footsteps ascending the stairs, he would whistle to him and receive a whistle in reply. The bird had quite a repertoire and always responded to the attention paid to him by repeating the sounds he heard. When the artist was busy and had not taken notice of his feathered friend for some time, the bird would pick up a piece of gravel from the bottom of the cage and throw it at him.

My recollections of Villa Fontana as it was seventy years ago are still vivid. It was an imposing three-story house with mansard roof and widow's walk, set well back from the street, from which it was hidden by tall evergreen trees. It was in one of Morristown's better residential neighborhoods, but at the time sadly in need of paint. The fountain, for which the house was named, was beside the driveway that led to the front entrance, but it was dry when I played in it as a boy. Large brown toads hopped about among the dead leaves that covered the bottom of the pool's big round basin. The heavy gate across the driveway was closed, and its hinges were rusty. It had not been opened since General Grant's carriage drove out in 1883. The inside of the house was somber, with curtains drawn in all rooms not being used. Certain memories of childhood remain very clear, and I recall especially the steamy atmosphere of the gas-lit second-floor bathroom as boiling hot water poured out of the faucet into the wood-encased, copper-lined bathtub, the height of elegance in Victorian plumbing fixtures. The fireplaces were surrounded by tiles depicting the artist's favorite Mother Goose rhymes and fables of Aesop. The motto "Time and Tide Wait for No Man," carved above one fireplace mantel, was beyond my comprehension but made a lasting impression on me.

Thomas Nast loved everything in nature, often staying up late at night to watch the stars and explain astronomy to his children. A story was told about the time he was sitting with a group before an open fire at The Players one cold wintry day and asked his friends if they would like to go out with him to see a great sight. Only one hardy soul cared to brave the weather. They had walked a few blocks when my grandfather stopped before a large plate-glass window covered with frost crystals. This was the great sight! His friend at first thought it was a joke but was soon convinced that Pop Tom was deadly serious; and he had to admit it was beautiful.

In his younger days Thomas Nast had enjoyed walking and horseback riding, although his riding days were over when I knew him. He loved animals, particularly cats, greyhounds, pugs, and terriers, as evidenced by their prominence in his drawings. When one of his dogs was poisoned, he was so distressed that he could not eat.

My memories of my grandmother, Sarah Nast, during these days are equally vivid. I recall her as a lovely, even-tempered lady who maintained her patrician bearing as she went quietly about her work presiding over the servantless Nast household. I never heard her speak a complaining or cross word, even during the later years when she was to make a home for me after my mother's death. I was fourteen years old at that time, and my grandmother was in her middle seventies. She saw me through a very trying period until I was ready to go away to college. I still remember the times when we were invited to dine with my Uncle Cyril and his wife, who lived nearby. I was a prodigious milk drinker; and in order to make sure that I enjoyed my daily ration, my grandmother would, to my embarrassment, carry with her a large pitcher of milk, holding it before her in order not to spill any as we walked along the city street together. Sarah Nast died at the age of ninety-two, outliving her husband by thirty years.

Would that I had asked my grandmother the many questions about my grandfather to which I would now like to have the answers. But as Catherine Drinker Bowen wrote in her delightful *Family Portrait*, one seldom begins to care about one's ancestors until reaching the age of fifty.

What bothered my grandfather most as the century came to a close was that he was heavily in debt. But he was not one to complain, even though he sometimes had to rely upon his talents to pay his doctor, dentist, and lawyer, by painting their

portraits for them. I was told that he once paid a tax collector in this manner, although how the collector settled with the taxing authority is not quite clear.

This lack of money was my grandfather's constant problem when, in 1901, Theodore Roosevelt succeeded to the Presidency of the United States. Roosevelt, himself a fighter for the things in which he believed, had long admired a similar spirit in Thomas Nast. So, wishing to do something to help him in his adversity, the President offered him an appointment as consul general in Ecuador. The offer was made in a letter from Secretary of State John Hay, advising that unfortunately this was

*Before he left for Ecuador, Nast posed with his unfinished portrait of the defeated Robert E. Lee. "One wonders," St. Hill says, "who looks the sadder."*
COLLECTION OF THE AUTHOR

*"Say the word and I am off," Nast scrawled on this picture he sent to Secretary of State John Hay as the time drew near to leave for Ecuador. He undoubtedly was aware that the golf bag he included in the picture was a touch of bravado.*

the only post available at the time. As Hay wrote:

The President would like to put it at your disposition, but if you think it too far away and too little amusing to a man with the soul of an artist, please say so frankly, and he will keep you in mind if anything better should turn up: but it is heartbreaking business waiting for vacancies. Our service is so edifying and preservative that few die and nobody resigns.

It was not an assignment that appealed to my grandfather, involving as it did business duties for which he was not at all qualified. But as he was desperately in need of funds, the four-thousand-dollar-a-year stipend seemed a godsend to the artist, who in his heyday had earned that much in a single month. He gratefully accepted the offer. It was a case of any port in a storm.

At the time he was notified of his appointment, Thomas Nast was working on a painting of the defeated General Robert E. Lee as he

awaited the arrival of General Grant at Appomattox Court House. It was to be called *The Hour of Surrender*. The painting was never finished, but a photograph was taken of the artist as he stood before his canvas, palette in hand. No doubt the disappointments experienced in later life had better enabled Thomas Nast to understand the anguish suffered by the great southern leader. Looking at the photograph, one wonders who looks the sadder, the artist or the General. It was the hour of surrender for both.

When the time drew near for his departure for Ecuador, the consul-to-be got off one of his clever sketches advising Secretary Hay that he was ready to leave.

Guayaquil, the principal port in Ecuador, where the consulate was located, had recently been ravaged by fire, and the climate would have been difficult for a much younger man to endure. Nast was sixty-one years old at the time. In addition, sanitary conditions were poor and yellow fever was prevalent. When a friend asked my grandfather why he was going to such a forsaken spot, he replied that he wanted to learn how to pronounce the name of the place.

One of the qualities that had contributed so much to Thomas Nast's success as a political cartoonist was his uncanny ability to foresee future events. The same characteristic was now apparent as he left for his new post. Among the sketches that he handed out to reporters as his ship was about to sail was one of himself shaking with trepidation as he stood on the red-hot equator, while "Yellow Jack," symbolic of yellow fever, popped out of a box and pestilential fumes poured out of a volcano in the background.

My grandfather departed from New York by steamer in July, 1902, convinced, as revealed in a sketch that he left behind, that he would never return. He sailed without friends or family to see him off. He

*This cartoon, which Nast drew for reporters as he left for Ecuador, was mostly a joke, but with his uncanny prophetic sense, the terrors he imagined were grimly accurate.*

could not bear the thought of such a parting.

The letters he wrote home to my grandmother were sad yet so revealing of his true character that it seems fitting to quote from some of them. Here was a man who had known the good things of life—a devoted family, a lovely home, a host of friends, and the esteem of his countrymen—living out his life in a pesthole in order to pay off his obligations.

Shortly after his arrival in Guayaquil in July he wrote to his wife:

I don't know what I am about, really. The fire, the yellow fever and the dirt do not help to clear one's mind.

Again, on August 3:

Things are really working very slowly. I have a bath but no water as yet. The cry is, "to-morrow, to-morrow," and their to-morrow is longer in coming than it is in the States. I am still well, but the people say here that I shall be laid up with a chill. . . .

They told me to be careful of the night air. Can't see how it can be kept out. There is not a pane of glass in the whole city. . . . The river is so close . . . when the tide is out the smell is in; when it comes back again it washes the smell away.

The picture of you and the grandchildren is up. As I look at it and see all laughing, I laugh too. It does seem funny that I am here, but my greatest happiness is that you are not here.

The picture referred to was a photograph taken in 1898 on the steps of the Morristown home. My grandmother, Sarah Nast, grinning like a Cheshire cat, is surrounded by her five grandchildren. Attired in sailor suit, with bosun's whistle in my pocket, I am seated in the front row between my two cousins Muriel Nast Crawford (the late Mrs. Donald E. Battey) on my right, and on my left, in ruffled dress and flower-bedecked hat, her brother, the late John William Roy Crawford, Jr., both children of Mabel Nast Crawford. Thomas Nast Crawford, the youngest of the Crawford children and the only one of us to inherit any

of his grandfather's artistic ability, is seated on his grandmother's lap. My sister Edith, eldest of the grandchildren, is on the right in the back row. She died of diphtheria two years later. It was a happy group, and little wonder that my grandfather laughed too as he looked at it. It added a cheery note to his otherwise dreary surroundings.

Two other grandchildren, Sarah Nast and Thomas Nast III, children of Cyril Nast, had not been born when this picture was taken. Thomas Nast III and I are now the only surviving grandchildren of Thomas and Sarah Nast.

Conditions did not improve in Guayaquil. On August 12 my grandfather wrote home:

Am well, that's all. . . . About four dead as near as I can make out, but the doctors say it was the genuine yellow fever. . . . Mice, rats, bats, mosquitoes, fleas, spi-

ders and dirt all thrive. I haven't had a real bath yet. There is not enough to fill the tub. . . .

Have to buy a bed, mattress, pillows, sheets and so forth, and set up housekeeping myself. . . .

Oh, the people are very poor. Times are hard—no work, nothing doing. I am so glad no one else came. . . .

How he must have yearned for the comforts of his home, including the water in his copper-lined bathtub!

And on August 21:

A month ago I took charge of this office . . . only a month—heavens! How long it seems! Well, I must make the best of it. I hate the place, but don't say anything about that!

Yellow fever was now so rampant that ships from the North carrying mail no longer stopped at Guayaquil. Sometimes they dropped off the mail on their return trip from southern ports. It was exasperating to the

*This picture of Mrs. Nast and their five grandchildren cheered Nast in his miserable life in Guayaquil. "My greatest happiness," he wrote Sarah, "is that you are not here."*

consul to see a steamer in the stream unable to put ashore the letters from home that he knew must be on board.

On August 27 he wrote:

It would go hard indeed for me if it were not for the Ashtons [Mr. Ashton was the British vice consul], because one needs somebody—in case—well—trouble of any kind. But I must not give in. If sticking will do it, stick I will. It does bring in more money than I can make at home and time may do something, too.

On September 15:

I think I am too old to catch the fever. I have a little hope left yet. Let's stick on for another year, anyway. . . .

September 21:

You say my poor old mocking bird misses me. I am very sorry. I do miss him, poor fellow, and his mocking sounds.

September 25:

This change has done me good in spite of everything. It is true there is a great deal of fever in this place, but I hope I shall escape it. They look at me and say "Well, you have not blue eyes. You are more like a native, and you are too old to catch it." What a blessing to be old. One is going to the next world soon, anyway, so one is exempt. For the first time I feel glad that I am old.

September 29:

Everything very quiet. The so-called "best people" have made their exits on account of the yellow fever. The steamers do not stop here. They go on south. That alarms these people still more. . . .

October 13:

Every day from two to four cases of yellow fever. Nearly all fatal. The Germans have the hardest time. . . .

I can save more money now as I don't have dinner at night any more. At first I had to, I was so hungry. . . .

Now that steamers had ceased to call at the port of Guayaquil because of the yellow fever scare, there was little for the American consul to do. His job involved representing his government in all matters of trade;

and when there was no trade, time hung heavily on his hands.

October 20:

Well, well, what with painting, when I am able to do it (it dries so slowly), and what with the Encyclopeadia Britannica I manage to kill time. I have been reading it steadily and enjoy it very much. Knowledge is a great thing, but what a nuisance to find out how little we know, no matter how long we live and how much we study.

October 21:

Your letter just came. You may say that you have nothing to write about, but write anything, even about the October days, the turning of the leaves. It makes me homesick, but I'd rather be homesick than have any other kind of sickness. Most of the people here look as if they were already dead. . . .

Then followed reports of several friends and associates who had succumbed to the fever.

And then came what was probably the saddest letter of all, dated November 21, 1902:

You say the money arrived safely and it is in the bank. Just think of it! Bills paid, and money, real money, in the bank again. . . . And so Mr. T_____ thinks I should get leave of absence from a

place where I am making money? No, I must stick it out, no matter what takes place. I do think I am making an impression, too, on the State Department. They have sent no complaints at all, and they may promote me, at least I hope so—and leave of absence would cost too much. I must stick. Now my job is all right, if we only get a little money ahead. . . .

How pitiful to think of the famous artist at sixty-two, hoping to make good on his four-thousand-dollar-a-year job so that he would be promoted.

On November 27 he wrote:

I am anxious to hear from you—something to be thankful for on Thanksgiving Day.

There was but one letter after this, a brief note on Sunday, November 30. The following day he complained of a little nausea, and by Saturday doctors pronounced his case as the fever in its worst form. On Sunday, December 7, he died, far from home and loved ones.

In his roll-top desk in the Morristown house was found the prophetic sketch made before his departure for Ecuador. It was a picture of his drawing materials, with his pencil and pen tied with black ribbon. ☆

*The poignant picture that Thomas Nast—once America's most powerful and famous cartoonist—tucked away in his desk*
Th. Nast: His Period and His Pictures

# American Gothic

CONTINUED FROM PAGE 33

travel, and scientific remarks upon *acoustics* from elderly millionaires who do not hear quite as well as formerly."

There were others, naturally, besides Davis, Upjohn, and Renwick who worked their Gothic will on America in the years between Jackson and Lincoln. There was, for example, John Haviland, the architect of stone prisons such as the Egyptian-style Tombs in New York. His most imposing work, designed in 1821, was the Eastern State Penitentiary at Philadelphia, which one local critic insisted was "the only edifice in this country which is calculated to convey to our citizens the external appearance of those magnificent and picturesque castles of the Middle Ages which contributed so eminently to embellish the scenery of Europe."

A fairly comprehensive Gothic tour would have to include nearly every state that was in the Union on the eve of the Civil War. If you happened to be an aficionado of the revival, you would not waste much time at Washington Irving's Sunnyside, for that heavily advertised villa at Irvington, New York, remodelled with the help of the artist George Harvey, has too coy an interior to please anyone who has surveyed the spacious plans of A. J. Davis. You would be more likely to linger over Roseland, the winsome frame cottage—Gothic inside as well as out—at Woodstock, Connecticut; once the home of publisher Henry C. Bowen, it is now owned by the Society for the Preservation of New England Antiquities. Roseland was the work of Joseph Collins Wells, the contriver of New York's First Presbyterian Church. Then there is Staunton Hill, the brick-and-plaster seat in Charlotte County, Virginia, of Charles Bruce. Now the residence of David K.

E. Bruce, our former chief negotiator at the Vietnam peace talks in Paris, Staunton Hill was designed by an engineer named John Johnson. And in Baton Rouge is the capitol planned by James Harrison Dakin, once a student in Davis' office; its central hall is overwhelming even today.

Harvey, Wells, Johnson, Dakin—these are names that only specialists would remember. Which makes it more than evident that the Gothic Revival was too popular to be merely the preserve of the leading architects of the nation. In fact, many of the most delightful Gothic remains are the work of artisans whose identity may never be discovered. No one knows, for example, who plotted the small but grim stone castle of the actor Edwin Forrest at Riverdale on the Hudson—now an administration building of a Roman Catholic college, Mount St. Vincent. Or who built the amusing frame cottage for John Schoolcraft, Jr., at Guilderland, near Albany. Or who thought of the unusual frame villa and teahouse of the California statehood leader Mariano Vallejo, in Sonoma, built about 1850 and now a museum. Nor is there much hope of finding out who slipped a Gothic veil sometime about 1850 over an essentially undistinguished brick dwelling in Kennebunk, Maine, making the Wedding Cake House a thing extraordinary. And although the records of William Gregg's mills at Graniteville, South Carolina, have been searched by scholars, no one has emerged with the name of the craftsman who made Graniteville a Gothic village.

To those who believe that the history of architecture is the history of common sense, the names of these designers may be facts not worth ferreting out. But architecture has always been an art of uncommon sense. A. J. Davis may have convinced more than

one client that the Gothic was ideal because of its associations. This was make-believe. Was it immoral? Had he not invoked the fourth dimension, time itself, he might never have accomplished what he did to make the plans of American houses flexible, irregular, and practical.

The Gothic Revival was, to use an accurate but ungraceful word, important. Born out of boredom with the perfection of the Renaissance and its emphasis on the proper proportions, it led to the rediscovery of the Middle Ages. When the monuments of medieval times were studied, architects could not help insisting that design and engineering, married so successfully at Chartres, should again be one.

There has, of course, been more than one Gothic Revival in the United States. When Ralph Adams Cram began preaching his crusade in the 1890's for churches that were monuments of archaeology, the Gothic of the decades between Jackson and Lincoln was dismissed as so much gingerbread. Commenting on the spontaneity of a Davis, an Upjohn, or a Renwick, Cram, the master builder of All Saints' Church in Ashmont, Massachusetts, left no doubt of where he stood: "The sheer savagery of these box-like wooden structures, with their toothpick pinnacles, their adventitious buttresses . . . and their jig-saw ornament, finds no rival in history."

There was, as we know, a time when Cram's Gothic was smothered with respect. Today he is only a bore to critics who insist that there was more to the toothpick pinnacles than caught his eye. In fact, Cram is so far out of date that there is serious danger he may be revived before the century is over. Taste would not be taste if it did not change.

*Wayne Andrews is Archives of American Art Professor at Wayne State University in Detroit. His next book,* Architecture in New England, *will be published by Stephen Greene Press in 1972.*

# Sway of the Grand Saloon

CONTINUED FROM PAGE 19

seasickness was entirely verbal: you simply told the victim—in a tone of voice implying that some slackening of moral fiber was involved—that it was all in his mind. Sympathy for the man or woman who is intractably supine and viridescent is, like gratitude, an emotion noted for its short term. Sometimes it has no term at all. Mark Twain, observing anguish all about him, handsomely states the case for those who are not only unsusceptible to the malaise but who also lack any shred of human feeling. Said Twain of his unfortunate shipmates:

I knew what was the matter with them. They were seasick. And I was glad of it. We all like to see people seasick when we are not, ourselves. Playing whist by the cabin lamps, when it is storming outside, is pleasant; walking the quarter-deck in the moonlight is pleasant; smoking in the breezy foretop is pleasant, when one is not afraid to go up there; but these are all feeble and commonplace compared with the joy of seeing people suffering the miseries of seasickness.

On the other hand Irwin S. Cobb's bout with seasickness made him philosophical. "As in the case of drowning persons," he noted, "there passed in review before my eyes several of the more recent events of my past life —meals mostly." To the elderly Canadian humorist Thomas Chandler Haliburton, rejuvenated by a voyage on the *Great Western*, seasickness was a frustration:

How I should like to make love, if it was only for the fun of the thing just to keep one's hand in; but alas! all the young girls are sick—devilish sick, and I trust I need not tell you that a love-sick girl is one thing, and a seasick girl another. I like to have my love returned, but not my dinner.

The distress of another early steamship passenger is expressed with sincerity and erudition. "I felt, rather than saw my enemy approach," he said. "He came upon a tall wave, with a white ensign, and a sparkling lance. His first blow was aimed at the very point of the system where the Ancients seated courage." When his ship—Cunard's paddle-wheeled *Asia*—came within sight of icebergs, his companions urged him to come see. He said:

But if each iceberg had been as radiant with gold and orange, green and violet, and prismatic generally as Trinity Church windows, with a Polar bear surmounting each glittering pinnacle, the scene would not have aroused my sense of the beautiful. If there is to be found beauty or sublimity upon the ocean, the mental tentacula must reach out and find it. But when they are paralyzed and shrunken by this everlasting sea-sickness —where is the sub—, I beg pardon. Eureka! It is the sublimity Burke discovered in Spencer's Cave of Error,—the *nauseate sublime!* Its monosyllabic expression is simply—Ugh!

The most drastic and costly measure ever taken to deal with seasickness was that by Sir Henry Bessemer, inventor of the process bearing his name by which steel is produced by the action of a blast of air forced through molten iron. On a cross-Channel trip from Calais to Dover in 1868 Sir Henry was overcome by seasickness of such an intensity that he suffered not only throughout the voyage but for the duration of the train ride up to London and into the day following his arrival home. His personal physician, alarmed, sat with him through the length of a night and eventually brought him around by administering small doses of prussic acid. The experience turned Bessemer's inventive mind "to the causes of this painful malady," which he— as did almost everyone else—mistakenly "attributed to the diaphragm being subjected to the sudden motions of the ship." The upshot was that famous contribution to the catacombs of pretentious curiosities known as the Bessemer Saloon.

In conception nothing could have been simpler: to isolate a part of the passenger deck of a ship "to prevent it from partaking of the general rolling and pitching motion," Bessemer built a model in which was installed a suspended cabin, supported on separate axes placed at right angles to each other. Pleased by the success of back-yard experiments under contrived conditions that he somehow thought were duplicates of conditions on the English Channel, he organized the Bessemer Saloon Steamboat Company and proceeded to build a pioneer vessel.

Patented in 1869, the finished product came out in 1873—a cabin of such proportion and appointments as had never before been seen on "the Silver Streak" (the English Channel). Seventy feet long and thirty feet wide, with a ceiling twenty feet from the floor, the *salon de Bessemer* was furnished with seats covered in morocco placed among carved oak divisions and spiral columns. Its wall panels, on which were hand-painted cartoons, were prettily touched up with gilt. It gave, said Bessemer, "an idea of luxury to the future Channel passage which all seemed to appreciate."

But nothing worked. The saloon refused to swing in a compensating direction, or sometimes even at all. To the assaults on equilibrium made by normal rolling and pitching it added the wild disorientation of a carnival ride. The first actual open-sea tests were disastrous, yet Bessemer was convinced that once he had got the bugs out so that his device could work at sea as smoothly as it had worked on land, a new era of salubrious water travel would begin. But ironically the vessel in which the saloon was contained turned out to be even more eccentric than the saloon itself, and Bessemer was robbed of his chance to prove his invention. At some crucial point in its docking maneuvers the mechanism of the Bessemer Saloon ship apparently refused to respond to orders. After banging into the pier at Calais on her first trip, the ship was repaired and made ready for a second chance. On this occasion, in May, 1873, Bessemer was himself aboard. He wrote in his diary:

We had arrived very slowly, it must be admitted—at the entrance of Calais Harbour. I, knowing what had occurred on a previous occasion, held my breath while the veteran Captain Pittock gave his orders to the man at the helm. But the ship did not obey him, and crash she went along the pier sides, knocking down the huge timbers like so many ninepins! I knew what it all meant to me. That five minutes had made me a poorer man by thirty-four thousand pounds; it had deprived me of one of the greatest triumphs of a long professional life, and had wrought the loss of the dearly-cherished hope that buoyed me up and helped to carry me through my personal labours. I had fondly hoped to remove forever from thousands yet unborn the bitter pangs of the Channel passage, and thus by intercourse, and a greater appreciation of each other, to strengthen the bonds of mutual respect and esteem between two great nations. . . . All this had gone forever. It will be readily understood that this second catastrophe at Calais finally determined the fate of the Bessemer Saloon Steamboat Company, which had thus become hopelessly discredited.

Bessemer died believing that his invention had not failed—simply that it had never really been properly tried. Over the smirks and laughter (an oscillating ballroom had slammed into France like a battering ram!) no champion arose to prove him right, no investor was willing to let him make another try.

Except by accident, or do-it-yourself voodoo, no one had yet been able to cure himself of seasickness. But the actual cause of it had been discerned,

and some ingenious if ineffectual means of dealing with it devised as early as 1870. In that year, an unknown writer defined the trouble succinctly:

The sickness is not occasioned, as is quite often supposed, by the mechanical effect of the motion of the ship on the digestive organs. The derangement of the system by the motion of the sea is primarily an affection of the brain, the affects upon the other organs being secondary and symptomatic; and the function of the brain through the disturbance of which the morbid action begins is what is called the 'instinct of equilibrium,'—that is, the instinct by which the mind, through some hidden action of the brain, takes cognizance of the relation of the body to the perpendicular.

Among the random and gratuitous kinds of advice for the victim were a number of ideas based on this diagnosis. "If qualms persist," said one authority, "pack the ears with gauze until a firm pressure on the tympanic membrane can be felt." When therapy by electric device was possible, someone invented a "seasick collar," by which to warm the neck and the base of the brain; and there was a related device by which the ear canals could be "toasted." The closest thing to Dramamine in its effects was probably the therapy offered by the medical staffs of the *Bremen* and *Europa* in the early thirties. This was the Dammert Inhalation Treatment. For fifty cents a go, this could be administered, to those in need of it, twice every day. As one advocate of the method said:

The patient who takes it lies down and breathes, through a nose-and-mouth cap, a mixture of oxygen and atropine. Atropine acts specifically to soothe the balancing system of the body which lies in the vestibulary apparatus of the inner ear, and once these centers are calmed, even a tottering great-aunt may become a trapeze performer.

To such instances of ingenuity old salts remained impervious and unconvinced. "The cure for seasick-

ness," said a commodore of the Cunard fleet, "is to separate the passenger from the ship." Yet one of the most remarkable things about the ocean was that its romantic attraction triumphed even in the teeth of its tendency to reduce the most ardent sea lover to a comatose bundle of bile. At its boisterous worst the sea for many people was a manifestation

of divine grandeur not to be denied by so trivial a thing as a man's organic disfunction. One of these wrote:

The solitude of a stormy night upon the ocean! What pen can describe! And yet who can be insensible to the luxury of that solitude—to its melancholy sublimity! And now as I write, our ship plunges and rolls in the heavy sea, and a death-like nausea comes over me. Our ship rises and plunges over these vast waves with much grandeur. It is majestically sickening, sublimely nauseating.

---

*In a forthcoming book John Malcolm Brinnin, a poet and professor of English at Boston University, surveys in lively and meticulous detail the history of passenger travel across the Atlantic.* The Sway of the Grand Saloon, *from which these two selections are taken, will be published later this month by Seymour Lawrence/Delacorte Press.*

# Liberty and Disunion

CONTINUED FROM PAGE 25

signs," unterrified by the spectre of prosecution for bigamy and adultery. In 1860 Greeley added that America must beware of the example of Rome, which, "under the sway of easy divorce, rotted away and perished—blasted by the mildew of unchaste mothers and dissolute homes."

Rome was much on the minds of conservatives in the booming post-Civil War era of expansion. The rush westward, the urban explosion, the rise of factories and a permanent working-class population, heavy immigration—all these seemed to threaten the homogeneous world of small towns and farms, and stable families, that had been America's strength. Fear was voiced that success would spoil the simple nation born in Philadelphia in 1776, just as empire had supposedly undone the virtuous republic of Cincinnatus. Rome's easy divorce rules, according to President Theodore Dwight Woolsey of Yale in 1867, were considered a special horror and warning to Americans by those whose anxiety rose with the revelation that the divorce rate was rising more rapidly than the increase of population. The actual numbers were not great (and statistics of divorce were, and to some extent are, extremely hard to collect and interpret). But a jump from just under ten thousand in the country in 1867 to over twenty-five thousand in 1886 was an alarm bell ringing in the ears of those who believed, with the Reverend Samuel W. Dike, of Auburndale, Massachusetts, that "the simple family of Christian civilization . . . one man and one woman, united in wedlock, together with their children" was the germ of villages, states, and mighty nations, and continually reproduced "the ethical history of man."

Action was necessary. Conservatives recoiled not only from the figures but from stories of divorces procured by fraud and bribery and from newspaper accounts of marriages broken up for what seemed light and transient causes—the "cruelty," to cite one case, of a husband whose offense was frequently reading Scripture to his wife to remind her, in St. Paul's explicit metaphors, of her duty of obedience. "Instead of resisting the erroneous and sinful inclinations of human nature," wrote one clergyman in 1892, "the State . . . surrenders to them almost without condition."

In New England, where forming improvement associations was almost second nature to worried intellectuals, a New England Divorce Reform League was founded in 1881. Four years later it went national, renaming itself the National Divorce Reform League, and in 1897 it broadened its activities to include assaults on "disreputable houses" and other threats to the chastity of both sexes and became the National League for the Protection of the Family. The league lobbied actively for toughening state divorce laws. It wanted longer residence requirements, the prohibition of rapid remarriage after divorce, and strict procedures for notifying defendants whose spouses had gone out of state to seek divorces and for giving them a chance to respond. It wanted high standards set for corroborative proof of charges of adultery or cruelty.

The league succeeded in getting a number of states to adopt such measures and appears to have slowed down the pace of divorce actions in some areas. In addition the league's tireless secretary, the Reverend Samuel W. Dike, worked effectively to get federal support for the collection of accurate marriage and divorce figures. And the organization launched strong efforts to create uniformity in separation procedures. It sponsored an interdenominational conference of 1903, which failed by only a small margin to adopt a united front against the remarriage of divorced parties whose original churches would not approve. (If adopted it would have prevented a Presbyterian clergyman, for example, from performing nuptial rites between an ex-Catholic and a Presbyterian.) The league was also behind a 1906 National Congress on Divorce Laws, which drew up a standard code that it hoped would be adopted by all states, so as to erase the dividing line between hard and easy jurisdictions. There was no sign of any widespread intent by state legislatures to comply, and the divorce reformers then tried to build unity by turning the matter over to the federal government through a constitutional amendment. This effort never got anywhere. One version of such an amendment was

fruitlessly proposed by Kansas senator Arthur Capper as late as 1947.

The gains of the league in some states, however, only enhanced the attractions of more lenient commonwealths, especially those where it was pleasant to linger. Divorce opponents could not wholly stamp out one of the oddest phenomena of American matrimonial history—the "quickie" divorce colony.

"The effort to base legal rules on moral and religious principles," observed Viscount James Bryce, "leads naturally to casuistry." In strict divorce jurisdictions that effort led to downright fabrication. Otherwise honorable men and women who could no longer suffer coexistence under the same roof went into court and "confessed," with pathetic willingness, to adultery, desertion, and other offenses in order to be freed. For those seeking migratory divorce, the truth stretching included a willingness to pretend that one proposed to become a resident of a new state, while the actual intent was to take the decree and decamp. In this prevarication migratory divorce seekers were encouraged by many communities whose Protestant ethic radiated contradictory messages. They respected the sanctity of the marital union. But they also wished to be diligent in their business and to collar any profits to be made out of marriage's decline and fall.

A modern generation, seeing the Midwest as the capital of corn, the seedbed of temperance and old-time fundamentalist religion, may have some trouble in visualizing it as the former locale of the nation's divorce capitals. Yet so it was. Indiana was the original divorce mecca, until its legislature, in the 1870's, tightened the residency laws. The best-known divorce center then became Sioux Falls, South Dakota, which showed great enterprise in profiting from those drawn to the state (admitted in 1889) by its mild divorce statutes and short residence requirement.

A reporter described the Sioux Falls scene in 1894. Each day's train was likely to bring a few wives who were ready to become the plaintiffs in divorce suits. (Wives usually were the complaining party in prearranged divorces—partly out of male gallantry and partly because they could be spared from business to wait out a three-month residence requirement, raised to six in 1893.) A new arrival would be taken to a good hotel, such as the Cataract House or the Commercial House; and before she had finished unpinning her hat, lawyers would be sending up their cards. Once she had engaged one, for a total fee of perhaps two hundred and fifty dollars, her task was to pass the time. If she was respectable, there was reading, shopping, and riding. If not, there were three or four gambling houses where lady patrons were not unknown. Though Sioux Falls had prohibition, there was solace in whiskey and brandy "tonics" sold by drug-

stores. And there were young men-about-Sioux Falls who gladly squired lonely and soon-to-be-single ladies of fortune. As soon as the waiting period was over, the new "resident" went to the courthouse of Dakota granite to file her petition and soon thereafter to testify privately to a judge that her husband was guilty of desertion, adultery, or cruelty, depending on what her lawyer suggested. (Somehow the details now and then found their way into the press, particularly if the divorcée was a celebrity like Mrs. James G. Blaine, Jr., the daughter-in-law of the one-time Secretary of State.)

South Dakota conservatives like Episcopal bishop William H. Hare were revolted by such proceedings. Bishop Hare led trainloads of protesters to the state capital to demand tightening of the laws. But Sioux Falls fought back, employing the classic argument that if it did not furnish a divorce locale other places would, and pointing out that in six months a rich and unhappy visiting lady could patronize merchants far more handsomely than local farm wives. A judge summed up town opinion when he declared that divorce seekers came for a lawful purpose, "as much so as if they sought the pure air and salubrious climate of the State for the benefit of their health, or its fertile soil for agricultural purposes."

Nonetheless, the divorce reformers finally got the state to lengthen its residence requirement to a prohibitive one year, in 1907. In that same year an attorney named William H. Schnitzer moved from New York to Reno and energetically began to call attention to Nevada's divorce advantages: the six months' residency, the lenient grounds, the private hearings where there was no contest, the privilege of immediate remarriage. Collecting these facts in a pamphlet, Schnitzer then took ads in Boston, New York, and Philadelphia papers. "Have You Domestic Trouble?" they asked. "Are You Seeking DIVORCE? Do You Want Quick and Reliable Action? Send for My Booklet."

Thousands did. Despite an eight-month suspension by

the Nevada supreme court in 1911 because of such solicitations, Schnitzer prospered. So did Reno's innkeepers, enriched by a rising number of divorce seekers, and in a newspaper jingle they reminded those who objected:

> If you legislate against the Reno Colony
> To other fields the fair ones you will drive
> For ill-advised propriety
> Brings poverty with piety
> And some of us would much prefer to thrive.

All Nevada, in fact, preferred to thrive. By the early 1920's the Reno court was granting a thousand divorces a year. (Las Vegas was then only a wagon stop between Salt Lake City and Los Angeles and did not emerge as a pleasure dome and divorce factory until late in the thirties.) Intoxicated with such success, the legislature in 1927 passed a bill cutting the residence requirement to three months. It went through at an all-night session, and a complaisant governor signed it before breakfast, and before conservatives could react. The result was all that enterprise expected. Reno, whose legalized gambling parlors were especially diverting to bored wives, was soon doing two million dollars' worth of business annually. Lush times were reflected in the sight of crowds strolling in "Alimony Park" across the street from the courthouse. (Alimony, however, was not an important factor in divorce history until relatively recent times. In 1916 it was awarded in only 15 per cent of all cases.*)

Then, in 1931, Reno met a challenge. Other states, sinking deeper into the Depression, determined to override scruples and bid for vacationing marital refugees. In February, Arkansas, already attracting tourists to its hot springs, reduced its residence requirement for filing divorce suits to three months, despite one Bible Belt legislator's cry: "It looks as if we have reached the same point reached by Judas Iscariot when he sold the Christ." The following month Idaho likewise cut its residence time to three months, and in 1935 Wyoming and Florida followed suit.

But Nevada's response was immediate. By votes of

*Originally derived from the Latin word *alimentum*, or nourishment, alimony was a payment required of husbands in the days when they were masters of their wives' property. If a husband received a bed-and-board divorce, he retained control of the spouse's assets but had to provide for her support out of their income. Time and feminism have changed the law so that men are no longer masters of their wives' wealth—but the obligation to support a divorced spouse (unless she is found to be the "guilty" party in a divorce) remains. While there are often good and sufficient reasons for alimony, many men are outraged at a pattern of past judicial practice which holds that in awarding alimony courts should exercise "a just liberality" with the ex-husband's means. Wives may receive alimony sufficient to maintain their former standard of living even from a husband thrown on hard times; they may receive it even when remarried; incredibly, some have even gotten alimony awards when "living in sin" with another man. For in the words of one judge who made such an award, the divorced woman owes her former mate "no duty to lead a virtuous life" in return for support.

34–0 in the house and 13–1 in the senate, the state promptly cut its residence requirement to six weeks. Forty-two days constituted a pleasant vacation amid purple mountain majesties and chattering roulette wheels, with board and lodging as low as twenty-five dollars a week at some dude ranches. Reno flourished more than ever as a result of its willingness to offer escape from what one ex-governor of Nevada called "the medieval divorce laws of other states." The 151 lawyers listed in its 1935 telephone book (in a city with only eighteen thousand permanent residents) had plenty of work, most of it undemanding, since 90 per cent of the cases were uncontested and a junior clerk could easily draw up the complaint. Fees averaged around two hundred and fifty dollars, and court costs under thirty dollars. Yet Renoites were slightly defensive. They liked to point out that their prosperity rested on easy marriage as well as divorce and that in 1934, for example, when 2,854 divorces were granted, 5,629 marriage licenses were issued. (Many, of course, went to brand-new divorcées beginning afresh.)

Other divorce centers rose and fell in popularity in the era between the two world wars. For the wealthy, Paris offered advantages in the twenties. The French grounds were broad (even to including "serious insults"), their judicial tradition was more interested in establishing facts than allotting blame, and until a 1928 tightening-up France's courts did not always probe deeply into the genuineness of a petitioner's declaration of permanent residence. Havana had a brief flurry in the thirties, as did the U.S. Virgin Islands—until the federal courts began to insist that a person who was claiming domicile in the territory would have to plan a longer stay than a Caribbean vacation. Mexico rose as a center for divorce after a 1914 law allowed its constituent states to set up liberal procedures. Chihuahua worked out a relaxed formula that required only one party to appear and establish "residence" by a simple statement of intent. If the other party consented, divorce could then be granted on several simple grounds, the least judicially agonizing of which was "incompatibility of character." The procedure took less than a day (with a Mexican attorney standing in for the absent spouse), and the time could be pleasantly passed drinking beer and shopping in Juarez. In that one city alone in 1934, 2,223 divorces were granted to foreigners. Twenty years later the total had reached 5,625; 4,300 went to Americans. (It was still rising in 1970, when Chihuahua suddenly made its laws more stringent, in a conservative reaction.)

Migratory divorce was not without perils. Each state of the Union is obliged, under Article IV of the Constitution, to give "full faith and credit" to the judicial proceedings of sister states. But there is a catch. The other state must be acknowledged to have lawful jurisdiction.

In many cases ex-spouses or heirs of persons divorced in out-of-state courts have sued to invalidate the decree by attacking the genuineness of the residence in the "foreign" legal domain. Sometimes they have won. The legal history of such cases is too tortuous for a layman to summarize without error. Suffice it to say that a husband or wife planning to get a divorce outside the home state would do well to consult a local attorney before buying tickets.

After 1945 statistics underscored what seemed to be a growing willingness to divorce, as an affluent and mobile population became impatient of pangs and frustrations once thought of as inevitable. A record-breaking number of divorces was recorded in 1946—682,760—as many returning veterans broke up unsatisfactory wartime alliances. In 1949 the ultimate bastion of conservatism, South Carolina, accepted the inevitable and adopted a divorce code. (New York, the other pillar, waited until 1966—but then adopted a liberal law that made voluntary, legalized separation for two years good enough reason for granting divorces.)

In the 1950's Florida, which offered sun, sand, and dog-tracks to the pleasure-bent divorce seeker, passed Nevada and granted an average of twenty thousand divorces annually, compared with ten thousand for the mountain state. A new and unusual divorce mill sprang up in Alabama, where sharp-eyed lawyers found that the residence requirement could be waived altogether if both parties acknowledged the jurisdiction of the state courts. A simple statement of intent to domicile from both parties allowed a judge to decide immediately that iniquities justifying a dissolution of the marriage had been committed. Before the Alabama supreme court, in 1964, cracked down on exploitation of this loophole, such celebrities as Hank Greenberg, John Daly, Grace Metalious, and Tina Onassis had utilized this brand of southern hospitality to be liberated from their spouses.

By 1970 the total number of divorces granted per thousand of population had reached 3.3, as against 0.5 per thousand in 1890. Yet those concerned for the future of marriage did not need to despair entirely. Divorce statistics are only an approximation of truth. Sometimes, it is true, they understate the actual rate of marital breakups. They do not, for example, show the hundreds of thousands of husbands over the years who, lacking funds or inclination to go to court, take the poor man's divorce, and desert. But on the other hand they sometimes paint a needlessly gloomy picture of social reality. Migratory divorces hugely swell the rate in easy jurisdictions—but over-all account for fewer than 5 per cent of the nation's separations. Or to take another instance, the most common ground for divorce in nineteenth-century America was adultery, with cruelty far behind—the reverse of today's situation. Were our forebears kinder, but more given to extramarital dalliance? Of course not. Adultery was then the most commonly acceptable grounds in court, and therefore the most frequently cited, truthfully or otherwise. Cruelty has become a more common plea in our time because courts are willing to interpret the word so broadly that it often means only incompatibility.

Whatever the future of matrimony in America, it can only be seen in a glass, darkly, in divorce figures. The American divorce rate has, in fact, been exceeded from time to time in recent years by nations as diverse as Japan, Algeria, Israel, Russia, and Egypt. In all these countries, as in this one, marriage is perhaps not so much in trouble as in transition. What is changing is a set of basic concepts about whose rights, in marriage, are paramount—those of the man, the woman, the children, or society. Finally, in the United States marriage is actually more popular than ever. Nine out of ten divorced people remarry, and a huge percentage of the new marriages endure until death. And first marriages continue to boom. In 1900 little more than half of all Americans over the age of fourteen were united in wedlock. In 1970 the proportion was up to 67 per cent for men and 62 per cent for women.

Marriage and divorce will undoubtedly take novel shapes in the age of the Pill and the abortion, to say nothing of other sweeping social changes. These new configurations will owe much, as they have in the past, to two factors. One is the universal human and social need both for marriage *and* for escape from marriage. The other is the unique mixture of traditions and outlooks that characterizes the United States' population in the third century of her national existence. In its own way, divorce in the land of the free will also continue to be as American as apple pie. ☆

# Disaster at Bari

CONTINUED FROM PAGE 64

tard in some manner," he explained to the shocked hospital officials. "Do you have any idea of how this might have occurred?"

Those who heard Alexander's statement that December day were stunned. After their initial reaction, however, they remembered a statement Franklin Delano Roosevelt had made in August, 1943, after he had been alarmed by reports of the imminent use of chemical agents by the Axis. In part the statement said: "As President of the United States . . . I want to make clear beyond all doubt . . . [that] any use of poison gas by any Axis power . . . will immediately be followed by the fullest retaliation . . ."

Was it possible that poison gas had been aboard one of the bombed Liberty Ships, brought to Italy for stockpiling in case it was needed? Alexander was determined to find out. If he was to save any of the victims still alive, he *had* to find out, and fast.

The British port authorities, when questioned, either did not know at that time or would not disclose for security reasons whether any of the ships carried poison gas. Alexander finally persuaded them to sketch the location of as many ships as they could recall, hoping that by correlating the deaths in the hospitals with the ship positions, he could narrow down his investigation to one or two of the Liberty vessels. He also alerted the military dock units to watch for any sign of chemical containers, had samples of the slimy harbor water analyzed, and ordered autopsies on the victims. His efforts paid off with dramatic suddenness when he received a telephone call from a British officer at the dock.

"We have just recovered a bomb casing from the floor of the harbor. It definitely contained mustard."

Shortly afterward, the bomb casing was identified as an American-type M47A1 hundred-pound bomb. The sketch of the anchored ships indicated that most deaths occurred near ship No. 1, which was identified as the American merchant ship *John Harvey*. Finally—and reluctantly—the British port officials admitted that the manifest of the *John Harvey* listed a hundred tons of mustard bombs, intended for storage in Italy in case they were required for retaliation after an Axis poison-gas attack. It was obvious that when the ship exploded, the mustard in the bombs was released. Part of it mixed with the oily water of the harbor, part of it with the smoke clouds drifting toward the city.

There were 617 recorded mustard-gas casualties among the military and merchant-marine personnel at Bari on the night of December 2, 1943, and eighty-four victims died. The full count will never be known, nor will the number of civilians who died from the mustard ever be learned. When it is considered that of the 70,752 men hospitalized for poison gas in World War I, only 2 per cent died, the disaster at Bari is put in its true proportion. Seventeen ships were totally destroyed by the German bombers, and eight others were damaged—the worst shipping disaster suffered by the Allies during World War II with the exception of the Pearl Harbor attack.

The Bari mustard tragedy was kept secret long after the end of World War II and is little known even today. It had far-reaching consequences, however. One lesson learned was the absolute necessity that those involved with the shipping of chemical agents should notify the proper officials immediately in case of a mishap or dan-

*Terror-stricken Italian parents carry a child hurriedly away from the area of the city where the German bombs first hit.*
WIDE WORLD

ger of a mishap. Very few of the mustard casualties need have died if their exposure to the poison gas had been known immediately. If the warning had been given at once, not only would the casualties have been treated differently, but many of the rescue personnel, crew members of the ships not sunk, and hospital personnel would not have suffered chemical burns as they did.

In addition, the action of the British officials made the situation worse. The British controlled the port, and they were extremely reluctant to admit that any Allied ship carried poison gas. Even when Alexander had proved beyond a doubt that the casualties were suffering from mustard exposure, Prime Minister Winston Churchill refused to permit any British medical reports to mention the mustard. The official reports, except for one or two preliminary reports issued before his ruling, stated that the burns should be listed as "NYD"—"not yet diagnosed." This restriction prevented medical staffs in many of the outlying hospitals, where a large number of patients were taken, from knowing the victims' true condition until too late, causing many unnecessary deaths.

Bari was the only major poison-gas incident of World War II. The tragedy was and is a grim reminder that all nations have secret stores of chemical agents ready for

The Sherlock Holmes of the Bari disaster was this American medic, Lt. Col. Stewart F. Alexander.
COLLECTION OF THE AUTHOR

use against each other if the need arises. The victims of Bari, those who died and those who lived, learned the horrors of chemical warfare. Even in an age when the nuclear bomb is the ultimate in weapons, poison gas is still a fearful threat. Let the user beware.

*Mr. Infield's article is based on his book* The Disaster at Bari, *published this month by Macmillan. He wrote another book for Macmillan,* Unarmed and Unafraid, *a history of aerial reconnaissance (1970).*

A personal tragedy in the mid-1950's led to my discovery of the Bari disaster. When my mother's illness was diagnosed as Hodgkin's disease, a form of cancer that originates in the body's lymph tissues, a local doctor told me that a new drug treatment was being used in a few hospitals in the nation, nitrogen mustard.

I made contact with the Sloan-Kettering Institute in New York City and promptly received from Dr. Cornelius P. Rhoads a reprint of a speech he had given to a medical society. "Dusty" Rhoads had been chief of the Medical Division, Chemical Warfare Service, U.S. Army, at the time of the Bari disaster, and the incident was mentioned as the ultimate source of the nitrogen mustard treatment for Hodgkin's disease and leukemia. My curiosity as a writer was aroused, and I immediately set out to learn more about it. Meanwhile, my mother was given the nitrogen mustard, and according to medical experts, the drug prolonged her life for approximately a year.

I soon discovered that even in the late 1950's the military were exceptionally reluctant to release any details about the poison-gas episode at Bari in 1943. I was rebuffed at the National Archives, where most of the available material was still classified. A letter to President Eisenhower, whose book *Crusade in Europe* mentioned the incident, brought a polite note from his military aide, but no more information.

I decided that to get the necessary facts I would have to go to the individuals involved. Dr. Stewart Alexander, the brilliant medical officer who determined that the mysterious deaths at Bari were caused by exposure to mustard, turned over his files on the incident to me and helped me locate other materials as well as people who knew about the event. Over a long period hundreds of men and women who had been at Bari sent me their stories of the tragedy.

In Europe I learned that even some of the "facts" that had been released about the incident were mistaken. For example, General Eisenhower's book indicated that the wind blew the mustard vapor away from the city, while citizens of Bari and military personnel who were there vowed that clouds of smoke covered the city like a blanket.

Through sources I cannot now reveal, I received the final official medical reports of the Bari incident, and these, together with a great mass of other materials gathered over years of research, enabled me to write my book.

The episode at Bari was a tragedy, but at least the medical knowledge gained from it is in use. That is some consolation.                                    —G. I.

urbs was accelerated by the automobile. Events appeared to justify the spokesmen for the advantages of the motor vehicle over the horse.

And yet, as current difficulties resulting from the massive use of the automobile attest, the motor vehicle's proponents were extremely short-sighted in their optimistic faith that their innovation would not only eradicate the urban health problems created by the horse but would also avoid the formation of new ones. As the number of automobiles proliferated and such cities as New York and Los Angeles experienced smog conditions that were a serious hazard to public comfort and health, it became apparent that the automobile, too, was a major obstacle to humane metropolitan existence.

Are the problems of noise and air pollution created by thousands of cars and trucks "worse" than those for which the horse was responsible? It is impossible to answer flatly. Altered environmental and demographic conditions in the city today, when judged beside those of a century or so ago, make specific comparisons between the horse and the automobile as polluters difficult at best. Aside from the disagreeable aesthetic effect created by horse manure, its chief impact upon public health seemed to come from wind-blown manure particles that irritated respiratory organs; from the reservoir furnished by the manure for disease spores, such as those of tetanus; and, most critically, from the fact that horse dung provided a breeding ground for the fly, proven by medical science to be the carrier of thirty different diseases, many of them acute. The pollution created by the automobile, on the other hand, is also aesthetically displeasing; and while it has not yet been firmly linked to any specific disease, it has primarily a chronic effect on health. The pollutants released by the internal-combustion engine irritate people's eyes and lungs, weakening their resistance to disease and worsening already present health problems. The immense number of automobiles in cities today has produced environmental difficulties that, unless soon dealt with, will generate problems that will dwarf those produced by horses in the cities of the past.

But the narrowness of vision of the early automobile advocates and their conviction that their machines would make urban life more tolerable, can be understood not as their failing alone. Most Americans, when informed of some technological advance that promises to alter their lives for the better without social cost, rush to embrace it. Second thoughts come later. Witness the apprehensions voiced presently over nuclear power plants after an initial flush of enthusiasm based on the hope that this cleaner and more efficient method of generating electricity would free us from dependence on dirty fossil fuels. We are only now learning to weigh the biological and other costs of new inventions with some caution. The career of the automobile has been one element in our education. Horses may be gone from city streets, but the unforeseen problems created by their successors still beset us.

*Professor Joel Tarr, of Carnegie-Mellon University, is an expert on the problems of America's emerging urban centers in the early 1900's.*

# "New York is worth twenty Richmonds"

CONTINUED FROM PAGE 80

dollars to repair. New York City had escaped destruction, but it was frightened and its mood was ugly. Had the plot been executed "with one-half the ability with which it was drawn up," said the *Times*, "no human power could have saved this city from utter destruction . . . the best portion of the city would have been laid in ashes." The *Tribune* asserted that "a catastrophe was imminent, without parallel during late years, and only to be compared in magnitude to . . . the great fire of London, the burning of Rome, or the destruction of Pompeii." "The wretches who would have destroyed all our principal hotels . . . by fire, and caused the death of their harmless occupants, deserve no pity," declared the *Herald*, "and should they be detected, as we have no doubt they will be, should be hung up in as brief a space as possible and as soon as the law will permit."

Saturday morning, as the early newspapers carried the first brief accounts of the night before, the Confederates were almost captured. They had assembled at the Exchange Hotel, near the Hudson River, where Kennedy and Chenault boarded, to size up the situation, and were seated in the parlor reading the papers when a burly man entered the hotel lobby. Martin recognized him as Sergeant John S. Young, head of the city's seventeen-man detective force. "Old" Young, as he was called, had spent the entire night going from hotel to hotel to alert proprietors and see that special watches were set up. He spoke to the manager of the Exchange and then sat down wearily on a banquette next to Martin, who was still wearing the federal officer's uniform. Kennedy, watching them from nearby, was certain they would all be caught and "expected to die then." However, after exchanging a few pleasantries with Martin, Young was summoned away by a patrolman, and the Rebels all breathed a sigh of relief.

Later that day Young set up guards outside ferry offices and railroad terminals in the hope of catching the plotters if they hadn't as yet escaped from the city. In the evening, however, the Confederates cleverly boarded a sleeper to Albany while it was still on a siding. As the car was pulled into the Hudson River Railroad station, they could see from their berths detectives on the platform outside stopping any suspicious-looking passengers before they were allowed aboard. Finally, at ten o'clock the train pulled out of the station, and after a stopover in Albany on Sunday the Rebels returned safely over the border to Toronto without incident, on another train.

Undeterred by his failure to capture the arsonists, Young accurately guessed that they must have been based in Canada. He persuaded both federal authorities and his own superiors to send himself and some of his men after them. Several detectives were quickly dispatched to Toronto; others headed for Port Huron and Detroit to cover the Canadian border with Michigan. Those sent to Canada were quickly able to worm their way into the confidence of one of Jacob Thompson's closest advisers by posing as southern sympathizers; they cursed Lincoln and spat on the Union flag to prove their loyalty. A meeting was arranged between Young and the Southerner. With amazing naiveté he fell for Young's ruse. The detective, feigning concern for the plotters, was able to draw from Thompson's

adviser an almost complete account of the plot; the city, he was told, "was to be wrapt in one dazzling conflagration." More important, the Southerner in all candor told Young that only six men had taken part in actually setting the fires. He said several were preparing to return south, by either running the northern blockade by ship or slipping through Union lines after crossing the Canadian border by train.

In spite of this information, only one of the Rebels was caught and tried. Kennedy, whose limp had been noted at several hotels, was easily spotted as he and Ashbrook purchased tickets in Toronto for a train bound for Detroit. A telegram was dispatched to two of Young's men there. They boarded the train as it stopped briefly at a junction outside the city. Ashbrook, who was sitting by himself in the same car as Kennedy, saw the two detectives as they were going from car to car looking for the Rebels; he opened the window by his seat and jumped out into the snow outside. The detectives failed to see Ashbrook escape, but they found Kennedy as he limped from the station once the train reached Detroit. He was arrested and returned to New York for trial by a military commission.

While in prison Kennedy wrote appeals for help to a number of Copperheads, McMaster and Benjamin Wood included, but each disavowed any knowledge about him or the plot when confronted by the police, who had intercepted the letters. Only circumstantial evidence was offered by the prosecution at Kennedy's trial, but the spirit of vindictiveness held sway. Found guilty of spying and of arson, Kennedy was hanged at Fort Lafayette on March 25, 1865.

Of the others, only Martin was ever captured, near the end of the war, as he was trying to help Jefferson Davis to escape. He implicated

himself by boasting to a fellow inmate in the military prison at Louisville, Kentucky, about his role in the plot. The other prisoner informed the authorities, and Martin was soon transferred to Fort Lafayette to await trial on charges of being a spy. By then the war was over, and no trial was ever held; a state supreme court judge ruled that since the writ of habeas corpus had been restored, civil law was again paramount to military law. Martin was subsequently turned over to New York authorities for trial on civil charges of arson; this time, a federal judge ruled that there was insufficient evidence to warrant the charges, and Martin was freed.

In the years after the war Martin became a tobacco merchant. He lived first in Indiana and then for several years in New York City before finally settling in Louisville. When the old war wound in his lung began hemorrhaging, he returned to New York for treatment, dying there in 1900. Headley joined Martin in Indiana for a while and eventually also settled in Louisville. He was secretary of state of Kentucky from 1891 to 1896. When last heard of, in 1905, Ashbrook was an insurance broker in Cynthiana, Kentucky. Harrington became a lawyer for the Southern Pacific Railroad and settled in Los Angeles. What happened to Chenault is unknown.

As for the mastermind of the plot, Thompson, he fled to England but finally returned to the United States, settling in Memphis, Tennessee, with much of his prewar fortune intact.

The night before he was executed, Kennedy, who had maintained his innocence until then, confessed to his part in the plot to burn New York. Had all his comrades "done as I did," he declared, "we would have . . . played a huge joke on the Fire Department. . . . We desired to destroy property, not the lives of women & children although that would of course have followed in its train." ☆

# POSTSCRIPTS TO HISTORY

## AMERICAN HERITAGE SOCIETY TOURS

Because of the American Heritage Society tours, which began this year, we are now happily receiving a whole new class of mail, and of a very rare and old-fashioned variety: thank-you letters. Our travellers clearly enjoyed what one, a teacher, called her "fantastic week of history." It left her "a bit overwhelmed and saturated but also impressed and satisfied." A rare-book dealer who joined in the same adventure writes that "From the Hudson to the Mohawk, Sunnyside to Fort Ontario, and the Waldorf-Astoria to Le Moyne Manor, the New York tour last week was continuous pleasure to me." Clearly, one of the main joys for our travellers was "getting behind the curtain"—avoiding the crowds, seeing things quietly, getting into interesting private homes, and being received as guests by curators, owners, even governors, all of them custodians in one way or another of the visible past. This month our second round of tours is underway in various parts of the country.

## OF ARMS AND MEN

After reading the article on Custer's Last Stand ("Echoes of the Little Bighorn") in our June issue, Colonel Alfred B. Johnson, of Alexandria, Virginia, questioned two points made by the author, David Humphreys Miller. The colonel said that, contrary to a footnote in the story of Joseph White Cow Bull, the Indians could not have captured repeating rifles during the battle, because the troopers were armed only with single-shot, breech-loading arms. He also expressed doubt about a footnote in the story of Dewey Beard that said

thirty-one soldiers were killed during the massacre at Wounded Knee.

The following is Mr. Miller's reply:

It is true that issue weapons of the 7th Cavalry, as noted in an ordnance inventory dated March 31, 1876, on deposit with the National Archives, were the Springfield .45 carbine and the Colt .45 revolver. Also noted were two Springfield .50 carbines issued to F Company, a part of Custer's immediate command; four Sharps .50 carbines issued to A Company and five to G Company, both under Reno's command; and five Sharps .50 carbines issued to B Company, under Captain McDougall, which guarded the pack train.

Although none but regulation arms were mentioned in later testimony regarding the battle at the Reno court of inquiry, where the orthodoxy of the weapons was apparently taken for granted by the military, it is possible, if not probable, that officers of the 7th followed Custer's own preference for unorthodox firearms. It is documented that he carried a Remington sporting rifle, octagonal barrel; two Bulldog, self-cocking, white-handled English pistols; a hunting knife in a beaded fringed scabbard, and a canvas cartridge belt. Mark Kellogg, accompanying the expedition as a newspaper reporter, carried a Spencer carbine, a repeating weapon; and the "Arikara Narrative" indicates that Custer's Indian scouts (at least the Arikaras) were armed with Colt's single-action army revolvers, and Spencer carbines had been substituted for the Springfield rifles first issued them. It is likely that the six Crow scouts, as well as other mixed-blood scouts and interpreters, were simi-

larly armed. . . . That some repeating weapons were carried by members of the expedition is substantiated by many of my Indian informants. . . .

Regarding Colonel Johnson's statement that I have created an erroneous picture of the Wounded Knee fight, I refer him to my book *Ghost Dance* (Duell, Sloan & Pearce, 1959), in which my reconstruction of the massacre at Wounded Knee is based on the testimony of twenty-one Indian survivors of the engagement in addition to that of Dewey Beard. On page 233 it states: "Yellow Bird and a few others who had guns put up a brief running fight." On the following page it states: "Within minutes all active resistance on the part of the Indians was over. Yet the troopers kept firing. Twenty-nine soldiers were killed outright in their own deadly crossfire. About the same number were wounded—two of them mortally." And on page 235: "Only one soldier was actually killed at Wounded Knee by an Indian. Captain George D. Wallace, commander of K Troop and a veteran of Little Big Horn, was struck down by a warrior brandishing a stone-headed war club. His skull crushed, Wallace was found dead near the council circle with four stray bullets in his body." As an officer, Wallace was not included in the death list of thirty-one troopers. Maps and description in the book show how the troops were disposed on three sides of the council area with additional troops dismounted as sentries completely surrounding it. Lack of discipline displayed by the troopers, by the way, so dismayed a young lieutenant in the campaign that he later instituted a new disciplinary code that was to last in the armed services for many years. The lieutenant's name was John J. "Black Jack" Pershing.

## A NEW LOOK

The interpretation of history, we are all aware, is ever changing. Wilbur R. Jacobs, a professor of history at the University of California, Santa

Barbara, now questions whether it is not the time to re-evaluate our ideas about the American West. Writing for the American Historical Association *Newsletter* of November, 1970, in an article entitled "Frontiersmen, Fur Traders, and Other Varmints, an Ecological Appraisal of the Frontier in American History," Professor Jacobs says:

Do historians have an obligation to help counteract harmful social attitudes about the environment that run contrary to the best interests of the nation at large? It is a question that has plagued the consciences of some of our best writers, including Francis Parkman and Frederick Jackson Turner. Certainly we historians have no responsibility for what has happened in the past, but we do have access to historic records and knowledge of what earlier generations did or failed to do. The public and students can expect, therefore, that we will make available the fruits of our investigations in a form undistorted by patriotism, prejudice, sentiment, ignorance, or lopsided research. But such a presentation of the American past is, in certain areas of history, not always the rule. This criticism can be applied particularly to specific subjects in "frontier" or "westward movement" history.

Historians of the American frontier, for instance, have failed to impress their readers with the utterly destructive impact that the fur trade had upon the North American continent and the American Indian. There are no investigations of the role the fur men had in killing off certain types of wildlife, which in turn had a permanent effect upon the land and upon native and white societies. The traders and their followers, the fur trading companies, are usually depicted as positive benefactors in the development of American civilization as it moved westward from the Appalachians to the Pacific Coast. Indeed, the story of the fur trade is almost always (and perhaps unconsciously) told with a capitalistic bias. The historian usually expresses a businessman's outlook in describing the development and expansion of this mercantile enterprise. If the fur trade contributed to the rapid economic growth of the country, and it unquestionably did

(Walter Prescott Webb argued that it helped to develop a boom economy in the first two centuries of our history), then the implication is the fur trade was a good thing for all Americans. Free furs and skins, free land, free minerals; it was all part of the great westward trek and "The Development of American Society," according to Frederick Jackson Turner and his followers. The self-made man, the heroic figure, who conquered the wilderness was the free trapper, the mountain man. Because the history of trading does not naturally attract the reader's interest, historians of the frontier have often gilded their flawed lily with a bit of spurious romanticism. The bear and bison hunter becomes the courageous tamer of the wilderness.

The real question of interpretation here is: who is the real varmint, the bear or the trapper who killed him? Aside from the fact that bears are sometimes noted for anti-social behavior, our frontier historians have not had a problem in answering such a question because their interpretations have been conditioned by a society steeped in a *laissez-faire* business ideology. Our view of progress—one which permeates all groups of society and leads us to accept without question the need for an expanding economy—is that progress consists in exploitation and growth, which in turn depends on commercialization and the conquest of nature. In our histories we have treated the land more as a commodity than as a resource. We have here in a nutshell the conquistador mentality that has so long dominated the writing of much American history.

## OUR ENGLISH COUSIN

Some historians not only look at the past but also try their hand at glimpsing what the future holds. Such a one is the famed British historian Arnold Toynbee. The following is an interview with him conducted by a scribe of the London *Sunday Times* who calls himself Atticus:

Professor Arnold Toynbee, who's currently revising his mammoth, 12-volume *Study of History*, must be our most controversial historian. His reflections on the

prophet Muhammed caused a riot in India in 1969 (four dead; 67 injured). "I was very surprised," said Toynbee. "I'm pro-Muslim." His *Study of History* brought some loud protests from fellow historians like Hugh Trevor-Roper. He called Toynbee's learned study a "windy soufflé" and accused him of egotism, obscurity and intellectual hanky-panky.

Toynbee, always amiable and never rude, refuses to shout back. "It takes two dogs to make a dog fight," he says. "Some critics aim to get your blood. Others aim at the truth." Where does Trevor-Roper fit in? "I really couldn't say," says Toynbee. "I met him afterwards, though and he was very polite. I can't remember what he said."

Toynbee's famous for seeing patterns in history and he says you can learn about the present by looking at the past. The Americans could have learned a thing or two about Vietnam by looking at the confrontation between David and Goliath. "Goliath was equipped with fantastic armaments. He would have been wiser to have taken note of what David was equipped with." . . .

Toynbee, who predicted the First and Second World Wars, is often accused of being pessimistic. He once said that the future of the world in the atomic age lay in remote places with people like the Tibetans and the Eskimos. "Unfortunately after I said that, the Chinese moved into Tibet and Western culture got to the Eskimos who started eating canned food."

He thinks our only hope lies in world government and unity by agreement. "In the past it's always been unity by a knock on the head which always seemed to work better." In the atomic age it's difficult. Everyone gets knocked on the head. Toynbee is still pretty pessimistic and he sees Black Power, hippy and drug cultures as possible symptoms of the disintegration of Western civilisation.

If he's attacked and called a windy soufflé in Britain, he's a revered figure in Japan. A national Japanese newspaper has asked its readers for questions to put to the wise Professor and Toynbee has just received a batch of 67 containing some like these: "What are we here for?" and "What is the nature of the universe?" Toynbee found them difficult but he struggled through. "I said something like: we are conscious of the universe but we don't understand it. . . ."

## THE WIZARD WINS

A photograph we ran in the April issue, that of Charles P. Steinmetz and Albert Einstein ("Dos Passos: The Wizards Meet"), occasioned a letter from C. P. Yoder, of Nazareth, Pennsylvania, who began his career in electrical engineering as a laboratory assistant at General Electric in 1910. Mr. Yoder, now curator of the Pennsylvania Canal Society, recalls:

The unique personality of Steinmetz, together with his genius as a mathematician, provided much meat for the publicity department . . . [from which] many exaggerations and myths developed. One much-publicized story that is no myth was his strong attachment to black stogie cigars. It is indeed rare to find a picture of Steinmetz that does not include his favorite cigar. Sometime prior to 1910 General Electric issued an order prohibiting smoking in the company's offices. When Steinmetz did not appear for several days, he was discovered working in his private laboratory at his home. When his absence was questioned, he merely remarked, "No smoking, no Steinmetz." Obviously, the order was quickly rescinded.

We reproduce above, in the next column, one of those rare photographs.

## SPOON RIVER: A CORRECTION

The editors regret that in the article by Edward Laning entitled "Spoon River Revisited," in the June, 1971, issue, we inadvertently failed to give credit to the copyright owner of the selections by Edgar Lee Masters that were used. Two poems that were quoted, "Anne Rutledge" and "Lambert Hutchins," are from *Spoon River Anthology*, the credit for which should read: Copyright ©1914, 1915, 1916, 1942, 1944 by Ellen C. Masters. The credit for the prose passage from Edgar Lee Masters' *The Sangamon* should read: Copyright © 1942, 1969 by Ellen C. Masters. We extend our humble apologies to Mrs. Masters, the poet's widow.

*Steinmetz, sans stogie, works on a problem in an unusual, but serene, setting.*

## THE LEGENDARY GOLDING

In recalling the adventures and the misadventures of an Army correspondent's life in World War II ("At War with the *Stars and Stripes*," April, 1971) our author, Herbert Mitgang, unintentionally omitted the role played by David Golding. Mr. Mitgang now adds this postscript:

In a remarkable group of Army journalists Golding served as a legendary managing editor for our Rome edition, which was generally considered to be the finest of the *Stars and Stripes* publications. A former reporter for a film daily in New York, he brought a hard-hitting Manhattan newspaper wisdom to military journalism and, with his movie experience, managed to juggle various prima donnas on the staff, most of whom wanted to cover the front line instead of sitting back in the fleshpots of Rome and Naples.

## A FEW THOUGHTS ON AMTRAK

For those of us who fondly recall and relish rail travel, the new government-operated railroad network known as Amtrak leaves much to be desired. Skepticism about the quality and frequency of service appears warranted, as the National Association of Railroad Passengers *News* pointed out in a recent article enti-

tled "Enthusiasts." Herewith, from that article, are quotations from three directors chosen by the nation's railroads to serve on the Amtrak board as the lines' representatives:

Louis W. Menk, chairman of the Burlington Northern, speaking on NBC's "Today Show" on February 26, 1970, said that "in my view we ought to let the intercity passenger train, the long distance passenger train, die an honorable death like we did the steamship, or the riverboats and the stagecoach and pony express."

William H. Moore, president of the Penn Central, told a news conference in Pittsburgh on September 9, 1970, that "probably all the railroads in the country are losing money in the passenger business" and that there is "absolutely no future in this country for long-distance passenger trains."

William J. Quinn, chairman of the Milwaukee Road, told members of the House Committee on Interstate and Foreign Commerce on November 13, 1969, that "we can no longer compete effectively for the passenger under present conditions, which are beyond our control to materially change," and that "there is no foreseeable reversal of this march of events which has produced an exodus from trains."

These remarks, all made before Amtrak came into existence, do not, we think, presage confidence in the system. The same NARP *News* quoted a member of its advisory board, Dr. Mario Pei, on the issue. Said Dr. Pei, who is professor emeritus of romance philology at Columbia University: "It is my considered judgment that the American railroad passenger system, once the finest in the world, is now on a par with underdeveloped countries, and in its death-throes. Also, that Amtrak is a snare and a delusion, designed to lull us into a false sense of security while the job of killing our passenger service is completed."

## A REBUTTAL

In "A Black Cadet at West Point" in our August issue, John F. Marszalek, Jr., claimed that a recent history of the Academy by Thomas J. Fleming failed to give a full account of the case of Johnson Whittaker, the black cadet who was investigated and court-martialled for alleged self-mutilation, among other charges. In *West Point: The Men and Times of the United States Military Academy* (1969), said Marszalek, Fleming "goes into some detail on the court of inquiry, but says nothing of the subsequent court-martial"; and Fleming was quoted as writing that although "the definitive truth will probably never be known," nevertheless, "any fair-minded examination of the case would find the evidence heavily against him [Whittaker]." This, Mr. Marszalek implied, is not a balanced view.

Mr. Fleming, who is a frequent contributor to this magazine, has sent us the following answer:

I did not discuss the court-martial of Cadet Whittaker in my book on West Point because, as Mr. Marszalek himself points out in his article, it was essentially a rehash of the court of inquiry. I am not at all impressed by the fact that Mr. Whittaker's court-martial decision was reversed. This was a political necessity for the Republican administration in Washington, who held office thanks to the slim majority provided by Negro votes. The Judge Advocate General may have "riddled the prosecution's case"—although I note Mr. Marszalek does not give us any details on this point. But the verdict was overturned on two technicalities, the lack of authority to call a court-martial and the introduction of Whittaker's letters.

Mr. Marszalek's article suffers from a severe lack of historical perspective. Nowhere does he tell us that Negro cadet Henry Flipper had already graduated from the Military Academy when the Whittaker case exploded. Nor does he mention James Webster Smith, another Negro cadet, who even Flipper admitted was a despicable character, who invited newspaper reporters to the Academy and told them malicious lies about his treatment. In short, there is no understanding of the glare of publicity on Negro cadets at West Point at this time, which makes the argument for Whittaker's self-mutilation much more plausible than the argument for an attack on him, which even the most prejudiced cadet knew would rebound on the Academy and bring the reporters swarming onto the Plain again. The whole theory of a cadet attack, in the light of the details, makes no sense. If they merely wanted to scare Whittaker into leaving, why did they tie him to the bed? Why not just beat him up a little, threaten to kill him, maybe clip off a little of his hair—but why tie him up so the tactical officers were certain to find out about it, and start a hue and cry? Anyone who has read my history and seen the innumerable anecdotes I collected of cadet ingenuity in evading tactical officer surveillance and rules, would scoff at such an idea.

I think Mr. Marszalek has been carried away by sympathy for Whittaker because of his treatment at the Academy, sympathy which, as I make clear in my book, I share.

## FIGURING AHEAD: *THE PASSAIC IN 1902*

Long before anyone ever heard of ecology, pollution was a problem. As far back as 1880 the Passaic River in northern New Jersey had lost its pristine quality. Pollution was the reason, caused chiefly by carbolic acid discharged by a paper mill and raw sewage dumped into the river by communities along its shores. As a result Newark and Jersey City had unusually high death rates from typhoid fever. Despite steps to control the worst offenders, conditions were not much better when the sardonic cartoons above appeared in the Newark *Sunday Call* in 1902. "How would you enjoy being a figurehead on the polluted Passaic?" the caption writer asked. "... it is to be hoped none of the craft that bears them will poke their noses further up than Newark Bay."

# THE REVISIONIST: *The War Party*

DRAWN BY MICHAEL RAMUS